OpenCV 3 Computer Vision with Python Cookbook

Leverage the power of OpenCV 3 and Python to build computer vision applications

Alexey Spizhevoy
Aleksandr Rybnikov

BIRMINGHAM - MUMBAI

OpenCV 3 Computer Vision with Python Cookbook

Copyright © 2018 Packt Publishing

Commissioning Editor: Richa Tripathi
Acquisition Editor: Alok Dhuri
Content Development Editor: Rohit Kumar Singh
Technical Editor: Ketan Kamble
Copy Editor: Safis Editing
Project Coordinator: Vaidehi Sawant
Proofreader: Safis Editing
Indexer: Tejal Daruwale Soni
Graphics: Jason Monteiro
Production Coordinator: Aparna Bhagat

First published: March 2018

Production reference: 1200318

Published by Packt Publishing Ltd.
Livery Place
35 Livery Street
Birmingham
B3 2PB, UK.

ISBN 978-1-78847-444-3

www.packtpub.com

`mapt.io`

Mapt is an online digital library that gives you full access to over 5,000 books and videos, as well as industry leading tools to help you plan your personal development and advance your career. For more information, please visit our website.

Why subscribe?

- Spend less time learning and more time coding with practical eBooks and Videos from over 4,000 industry professionals

- Improve your learning with Skill Plans built especially for you

- Get a free eBook or video every month

- Mapt is fully searchable

- Copy and paste, print, and bookmark content

PacktPub.com

Did you know that Packt offers eBook versions of every book published, with PDF and ePub files available? You can upgrade to the eBook version at `www.PacktPub.com` and as a print book customer, you are entitled to a discount on the eBook copy. Get in touch with us at `service@packtpub.com` for more details.

At `www.PacktPub.com`, you can also read a collection of free technical articles, sign up for a range of free newsletters, and receive exclusive discounts and offers on Packt books and eBooks.

Contributors

About the authors

Alexey Spizhevoy has over 7 years of experience in computer vision R&D. He has worked for 5 years at Itseez, the main OpenCV contributor, before it was acquired by Intel. He has contributed to video stabilization and photo stitching modules into OpenCV library. He has successfully participated in numerous Computer Vision projects in such areas as 3D reconstruction, video conferencing, object detection and tracking, semantic segmentation, driving assistance, and others. He holds a master's degree in computer science, and he is currently pursuing PhD.

Aleksandr Rybnikov has over 5 years of experience in C++ programming, including 3 years in the **Computer Vision (CV)** domain. He worked at Itseez, a company that supported and developed OpenCV, and then at Intel. He enriched OpenCV's dnn module by adding support of another two **Deep Learning (DL)** frameworks and many features, along with improving the existing functionality. As an engineer, he participated in CV and DL projects such as iris recognition, object detection, semantic segmentation, 6-DOF pose estimation, and digital hologram reconstruction. He has a master's degree in physics.

Without the great teachers I had, this book wouldn't have been possible. So I want to express gratitude to my colleagues who guided and advised me on my path in Computer Vision. Writing a book, especially when you want to make it useful and practical, isn't simple in any way and takes a lot of time. Many thanks and love to my wife, Daria Tikhonova, who has supported me while working on the book.

About the reviewer

Joseph Howse lives in a Canadian fishing village with four cats; the cats like fish, but they prefer chicken.

Joseph provides computer vision expertise through his company, Nummist Media. He is a Packt author whose books include *OpenCV for Secret Agents*, *OpenCV 3 Blueprints*, *Android Application Programming with OpenCV 3*, *iOS Application Development with OpenCV 3*, *Learning OpenCV 3 Computer Vision with Python*, and *Python Game Programming by Example*.

> *I wish to congratulate this book's authors, who have contributed so much code and wisdom to the OpenCV community. I am also thankful to the whole team at Packt for our continued collaboration. As always, I dedicate my work to Sam, Jan, Bob, Bunny, and the cats.*

Packt is searching for authors like you

If you're interested in becoming an author for Packt, please visit `authors.packtpub.com` and apply today. We have worked with thousands of developers and tech professionals, just like you, to help them share their insight with the global tech community. You can make a general application, apply for a specific hot topic that we are recruiting an author for, or submit your own idea.

Table of Contents

Preface

Computer Vision is a broad topic comprising a lot of different areas. If you want to start using Computer Vision algorithms in your projects, it may be ambiguous where the entry point is. Even if you're an experienced Computer Vision engineer, undoubtedly there are some technologies that you would want to explore in depth or get familiar with. In both cases, a practical approach works best. Only through applying methods to real problems, tuning existing methods to meet your requirements, and playing with samples can you fully understand the possibilities and limitations of any Computer Vision algorithm. This book is specifically designed to get your hands dirty with solving real computer vision tasks. Recipes in this book use OpenCV—the most popular, functionally rich, and widely used open source Computer Vision library. This book progresses from the simplest samples to the most complicated ones, so you will be able to find some useful and information which is easy to understand.

Who this book is for

This book is for developers who have basic knowledge of Python. If you are aware of the basics of OpenCV and are ready to build computer vision systems that are smarter, faster, more complex, and more practical than the competition, then this book is for you.

What this book covers

Chapter 1, *I/O and GUI*, teaches the basic operations with images and video: loading, saving and displaying.

Chapter 2, *Matrices, Colors, and Filters*, covers operations to manipulate with matrices: accessing regions of an image, channels, and pixels. Conversions between various color spaces and usage of filters are also described.

Chapter 3, *Contours and Segmentation*, shows how to create image masks, find contours, and segment images.

Chapter 4, *Object Detection and Machine Learning*, describes ways of detecting and tracking different types of objects, from specially constructed (QR codes and ArUCo markers) to ones that can be met in natural scenes.

Chapter 5, *Deep Learning*, outlines new functionality in OpenCV connected with Deep Neural Nets. It provides examples of loading Deep Learning models and applying them to Computer Vision tasks.

Chapter 6, *Linear Algebra*, dives into useful mathematical methods for solving linear algebra problems and provides examples of applying these methods in Computer Vision.

Chapter 7, *Detectors and Descriptors*, contains information about how to work with image feature descriptors: how to compute them with different methods, how to display them, and how to match them for object detection and tracking purposes.

Chapter 8, *Image and Video Processing*, shows readers how to work with image sequences and get results based on correlations among the sequence.

Chapter 9, *Multiple View Geometry*, describes how to use cameras to retrieve information about 3D geometry of the scene.

To get the most out of this book

All the required information to get started with the respective recipes is mentioned in the recipes.

Download the example code files

You can download the example code files for this book from your account at www.packtpub.com. If you purchased this book elsewhere, you can visit www.packtpub.com/support and register to have the files emailed directly to you.

You can download the code files by following these steps:

1. Log in or register at www.packtpub.com.
2. Select the **SUPPORT** tab.
3. Click on **Code Downloads & Errata**.
4. Enter the name of the book in the **Search** box and follow the onscreen instructions.

Once the file is downloaded, please make sure that you unzip or extract the folder using the latest version of:

- WinRAR/7-Zip for Windows
- Zipeg/iZip/UnRarX for Mac
- 7-Zip/PeaZip for Linux

The code bundle for the book is also hosted on GitHub at `https://github.com/PacktPublishing/OpenCV-3-Computer-Vision-with-Python-Cookbook`. In case there's an update to the code, it will be updated on the existing GitHub repository.

We also have other code bundles from our rich catalog of books and videos available at `https://github.com/PacktPublishing/`. Check them out!

Download the color images

We also provide a PDF file that has color images of the screenshots/diagrams used in this book. You can download it here: `https://www.packtpub.com/sites/default/files/downloads/OpenCV3ComputerVisionwithPythonCookbook_ColorImages.pdf`.

Conventions used

There are a number of text conventions used throughout this book.

`CodeInText`: Indicates code words in text, database table names, folder names, filenames, file extensions, pathnames, dummy URLs, user input, and Twitter handles. Here is an example: "The `cv2.flip` function is used for mirroring images."

A block of code is set as follows:

```
import argparse
import cv2
parser = argparse.ArgumentParser()
parser.add_argument('--path', default='../data/Lena.png', help='Image
path.')
params = parser.parse_args()
img = cv2.imread(params.path)
```

When we wish to draw your attention to a particular part of a code block, the relevant lines or items are set in bold:

```
import argparse
import cv2
parser = argparse.ArgumentParser()
parser.add_argument('--path', default='../data/Lena.png', help='Image
path.')
params = parser.parse_args()
img = cv2.imread(params.path)
```

Any command-line input or output is written as follows:

```
read ../data/Lena.png
shape: (512, 512, 3)
dtype: uint8

read ../data/Lena.png as grayscale
shape: (512, 512)
dtype: uint8
```

Bold: Indicates a new term, an important word, or words that you see onscreen.

Warnings or important notes appear like this.

Tips and tricks appear like this.

Sections

In this book, you will find several headings that appear frequently (*Getting ready, How to do it..., How it works..., There's more...,* and *See also*).

To give clear instructions on how to complete a recipe, use these sections as follows:

Getting ready

This section tells you what to expect in the recipe and describes how to set up any software or any preliminary settings required for the recipe.

How to do it...

This section contains the steps required to follow the recipe.

How it works...

This section usually consists of a detailed explanation of what happened in the previous section.

There's more...

This section consists of additional information about the recipe in order to make you more knowledgeable about the recipe.

See also

This section provides helpful links to other useful information for the recipe.

Get in touch

Feedback from our readers is always welcome.

General feedback: Email `feedback@packtpub.com` and mention the book title in the subject of your message. If you have questions about any aspect of this book, please email us at `questions@packtpub.com`.

Errata: Although we have taken every care to ensure the accuracy of our content, mistakes do happen. If you have found a mistake in this book, we would be grateful if you would report this to us. Please visit `www.packtpub.com/submit-errata`, selecting your book, clicking on the Errata Submission Form link, and entering the details.

Piracy: If you come across any illegal copies of our works in any form on the internet, we would be grateful if you would provide us with the location address or website name. Please contact us at `copyright@packtpub.com` with a link to the material.

If you are interested in becoming an author: If there is a topic that you have expertise in and you are interested in either writing or contributing to a book, please visit `authors.packtpub.com`.

Reviews

Please leave a review. Once you have read and used this book, why not leave a review on the site that you purchased it from? Potential readers can then see and use your unbiased opinion to make purchase decisions, we at Packt can understand what you think about our products, and our authors can see your feedback on their book. Thank you!

For more information about Packt, please visit `packtpub.com`.

1
I/O and GUI

In this chapter, we will cover the following recipes:

- Reading images from file
- Simple image transformations—resizing and flipping
- Saving images using lossy and lossless compression
- Showing images in an OpenCV window
- Working with UI elements, such as buttons and trackbars, in an OpenCV window
- Drawing 2D primitives—markers, lines, ellipses, rectangles, and text
- Handling user input from a keyboard
- Making your app interactive through handling user input from a mouse
- Capturing and showing frames from a camera
- Playing frame stream from video
- Obtaining a frame stream properties
- Writing a frame stream into video
- Jumping between frames in video files

Introduction

Computer vision algorithms consume and produce data—they usually take images as an input and generate features of the input, such as contours, points or regions of interest, bounding boxes for objects, or another images. So dealing with the input and output of graphical information is an essential part of any computer vision algorithm. This means not only reading and saving images, but also displaying them with additional information about their features.

In this chapter, we will cover basic OpenCV functionality related to I/O functions. From the recipes, you will learn how to obtain images from different sources (either filesystem or camera), display them, and save images and videos. Also, the chapter covers the topic of working with the OpenCV UI system; for instance, in creating windows and trackbars.

Reading images from files

In this recipe, we will learn how to read images from files. OpenCV supports reading images in different formats, such as PNG, JPEG, and TIFF. Let's write a program that takes the path to an image as its first parameter, reads the image, and prints its shape and size.

Getting ready

You need to have OpenCV 3.x installed with Python API support.

How to do it...

For this recipe, you need to perform the following steps:

1. You can easily read an image with the `cv2.imread` function, which takes path to image and optional flags:

```
import argparse
import cv2
parser = argparse.ArgumentParser()
parser.add_argument('--path', default='../data/Lena.png',
help='Image path.')
params = parser.parse_args()
img = cv2.imread(params.path)
```

2. Sometimes it's useful to check whether the image was successfully loaded or not:

```
assert img is not None  # check if the image was successfully
loaded
print('read {}'.format(params.path))
print('shape:', img.shape)
print('dtype:', img.dtype)
```

3. Load the image and convert it to grayscale, even if it had many color channels originally:

```
img = cv2.imread(params.path, cv2.IMREAD_GRAYSCALE)
assert img is not None
print('read {} as grayscale'.format(params.path))
print('shape:', img.shape)
print('dtype:', img.dtype)
```

How it works...

The loaded image is represented as a NumPy array. The same representation is used in OpenCV for matrices. NumPy arrays have such properties as shape, which is an image's size and number of color channels, and dtype, which is the underlying data type (for example, uint8 or float32). Note that OpenCV loads images in BGR, not RGB, format.

The shape tuple in this case should be interpreted as follows: image height, image width, color channels count.

The cv.imread function also supports optional flags, where users can specify whether conversion to uint8 type should be performed, and whether the image is grayscale or color.

Having run the code with the default parameters, you should see the following output:

```
read ../data/Lena.png
shape: (512, 512, 3)
dtype: uint8

read ../data/Lena.png as grayscale
shape: (512, 512)
dtype: uint8
```

Simple image transformations—resizing and flipping

Now we're able to load an image, it's time to do some simple image processing. The operations we're going to review—resize and flip—are basic and usually used as preliminary steps of complex computer vision algorithms.

Getting ready

You need to have OpenCV 3.x installed with Python API support.

How to do it...

For this recipe, we need the following steps to be executed:

1. Load an image and print its original size:

```
img = cv2.imread('../data/Lena.png')
print('original image shape:', img.shape)
```

2. OpenCV offers several ways of using the `cv2.resize` function. We can set the target size (`width`, `height`) in pixels as the second parameter:

```
width, height = 128, 256
resized_img = cv2.resize(img, (width, height))
print('resized to 128x256 image shape:', resized_img.shape)
```

3. Resize by setting multipliers of the image's original width and height:

```
w_mult, h_mult = 0.25, 0.5
resized_img = cv2.resize(img, (0, 0), resized_img, w_mult, h_mult)
print('image shape:', resized_img.shape)
```

4. Resize using nearest-neighbor interpolation instead of the default one:

```
w_mult, h_mult = 2, 4
resized_img = cv2.resize(img, (0, 0), resized_img, w_mult, h_mult,
cv2.INTER_NEAREST)
print('half sized image shape:', resized_img.shape)
```

5. Reflect the image along its horizontal *x*-axis. To do this, we should pass 0 as the last argument of the `cv2.flip` function:

```
img_flip_along_x = cv2.flip(img, 0)
```

6. Of course, it's possible to flip the image along its vertical *y*-axis—just pass any value greater than 0:

```
img_flip_along_y = cv2.flip(img, 1)
```

7. We can flip both *x* and *y* simultaneously by passing any negative value to the function:

```
img_flipped_xy = cv2.flip(img, -1)
```

How it works...

We can play with interpolation mode in `cv2.resize`—it defines how values between pixels are computed. There are quite a few types of interpolation, each with a different outcome. This argument can be passed as the last one and doesn't influence the result's size—only the quality and smoothness of the output.

By default, bilinear interpolation (`cv2.INTER_LINEAR`) is used. But in some situations, it may be necessary to apply other, more complicated options.

The `cv2.flip` function is used for mirroring images. It doesn't change the size of an image, but rather swaps the pixels.

Saving images using lossy and lossless compression

This recipe will teach you how to save images. Sometimes you want to get feedback from your computer vision algorithm. One way to do so is to store results on a disk. The feedback could be final images, pictures with additional information such as contours, metrics, values and so on, or results of individual steps from a complicated pipeline.

Getting ready

You need to have OpenCV 3.x installed with Python API support.

How to do it...

Here are the steps for this recipe:

1. First, read the image:

```
img = cv2.imread('../data/Lena.png')
```

2. Save the image in PNG format without losing quality, then read it again to check whether all the information has been preserved during writing onto the disk:

```
# save image with lower compression—bigger file size but faster
decoding
cv2.imwrite('../data/Lena_compressed.png', img,
[cv2.IMWRITE_PNG_COMPRESSION, 0])

# check that image saved and loaded again image is the same as
original one
saved_img = cv2.imread(params.out_png)
assert saved_img.all() == img.all()
```

3. Save the image in the JPEG format:

```
# save image with lower quality—smaller file size
cv2.imwrite('../data/Lena_compressed.jpg', img,
[cv2.IMWRITE_JPEG_QUALITY, 0])
```

How it works...

To save an image, you should use the `cv2.imwrite` function. The file's format is determined by this function, as can be seen in the filename (JPEG, PNG, and some others are supported). There are two main options for saving images: whether to lose some information while saving, or not.

The `cv2.imwrite` function takes three arguments: the path of output file, the image itself, and the parameters of saving. When saving an image to PNG format, we can specify the compression level. The value of `IMWRITE_PNG_COMPRESSION` must be in the (0, 9) interval—the bigger the number, the smaller the file on the disk, but the slower the decoding process.

When saving to JPEG format, we can manage the compression process by setting the value of `IMWRITE_JPEG_QUALITY`. We can set this as any value from 0 to 100. But here, we have a situation where bigger is better. Larger values lead to higher result quality and a lower amount of JPEG artifacts.

Showing images in an OpenCV window

One of the many brilliant features of OpenCV is that you can visualize images with very little effort. Here we will learn all about showing images in OpenCV.

Getting ready

You need to have OpenCV 3.x installed with Python API support.

How to do it...

The steps are as follows:

1. Load an image to have something to work with and get its size:

    ```
    orig = cv2.imread('../data/Lena.png')
    orig_size = orig.shape[0:2]
    ```

2. Now let's display our image. To do so, we need to call the `cv2.imshow` and `cv2.waitKey` functions:

    ```
    cv2.imshow("Original image", orig)
    cv2.waitKey(2000)
    ```

How it works...

Now, let's shed some light on the functions. The `cv2.imshow` function is needed to show the image—its first parameter is the name of the window (see the header of the window in the following screenshot), the second parameter is the image we want to display. The `cv2.waitKey` function is necessary for controlling the display time of the window.

Note that the display time must be explicitly controlled, otherwise you won't see any windows. The function takes the duration of the window display time in milliseconds. But if you press any key on the keyboard, the window will disappear earlier than the specified time. We will review this functionality in one of the following recipes.

The code above results in the following:

Working with UI elements, such as buttons and trackbars, in an OpenCV window

In this recipe, we will learn how to add UI elements, such as buttons and trackbars, into OpenCV windows and work with them. Trackbars are useful UI elements that:

- Show the value of an integer variable, assuming the value is within a predefined range
- Allow us to change the value interactively through changing the trackbar position

Let's create a program that allows users to specify the fill color for an image by interactively changing each **Red**, **Green**, **Blue** (**RGB**) channel value.

Getting ready

You need to have OpenCV 3.x installed with Python API support.

How to do it...

To complete this recipe, the steps are as follows:

1. First create an OpenCV window named `window`:

```
import cv2, numpy as np

cv2.namedWindow('window')
```

2. Create a variable that will contain the fill color value for the image. The variable is a NumPy array with three values that will be interpreted as blue, green, and red color components (in that order) from the [0, 255] range:

```
fill_val = np.array([255, 255, 255], np.uint8)
```

3. Add an auxiliary function to call from each `trackbar_callback` function. The function takes the color component index and new value as settings:

```
def trackbar_callback(idx, value):
    fill_val[idx] = value
```

4. Add three trackbars into `window` and bind each trackbar callback to a specific color component using the Python `lambda` function:

```
cv2.createTrackbar('R', 'window', 255, 255, lambda v:
trackbar_callback(2, v))
cv2.createTrackbar('G', 'window', 255, 255, lambda v:
trackbar_callback(1, v))
cv2.createTrackbar('B', 'window', 255, 255, lambda v:
trackbar_callback(0, v))
```

5. In a loop, show the image in a window with three trackbars and process keyboard input as well:

```
while True:
    image = np.full((500, 500, 3), fill_val)
    cv2.imshow('window', image)
    key = cv2.waitKey(3)
    if key == 27:
        break
cv2.destroyAllWindows()
```

How it works...

A window like the one following is expected to be shown, though it might vary slightly depending on the version of OpenCV and how it was built:

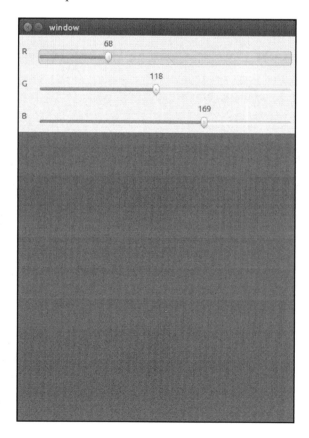

Drawing 2D primitives—markers, lines, ellipses, rectangles, and text

Just after you implement your first computer vision algorithm, you will want to see its results. OpenCV has a considerable number of drawing functions to let you highlight any feature in an image.

Getting ready

You need to have OpenCV 3.x installed with Python API support.

How to do it...

1. Open an image and get its width and height. Also, define a simple function that returns a random point inside our image:

```
import cv2, random

image = cv2.imread('../data/Lena.png')
w, h = image.shape[1], image.shape[0]


def rand_pt(mult=1.):
    return (random.randrange(int(w*mult)),
            random.randrange(int(h*mult)))
```

2. Let's draw something! Let's go for circles:

```
cv2.circle(image, rand_pt(), 40, (255, 0, 0))
cv2.circle(image, rand_pt(), 5, (255, 0, 0), cv2.FILLED)
cv2.circle(image, rand_pt(), 40, (255, 85, 85), 2)
cv2.circle(image, rand_pt(), 40, (255, 170, 170), 2, cv2.LINE_AA)
```

3. Now let's try to draw lines:

```
cv2.line(image, rand_pt(), rand_pt(), (0, 255, 0))
cv2.line(image, rand_pt(), rand_pt(), (85, 255, 85), 3)
cv2.line(image, rand_pt(), rand_pt(), (170, 255, 170), 3,
cv2.LINE_AA)
```

4. If you want to draw an arrow, use the `arrowedLine()` function:

```
cv2.arrowedLine(image, rand_pt(), rand_pt(), (0, 0, 255), 3,
cv2.LINE_AA)
```

5. To draw rectangles, OpenCV has the `rectangle()` function:

```
cv2.rectangle(image, rand_pt(), rand_pt(), (255, 255, 0), 3)
```

6. Also, OpenCV includes a function to draw ellipses. Let's draw them:

```
cv2.ellipse(image, rand_pt(), rand_pt(0.3), random.randrange(360),
0, 360, (255, 255, 255), 3)
```

7. Our final drawing-related function is for placing text on the image:

```
cv2.putText(image, 'OpenCV', rand_pt(), cv2.FONT_HERSHEY_SIMPLEX,
1, (0, 0, 0), 3)
```

How it works...

First, `cv2.circle` gives the thinnest and darkest blue primitive. The second invocation draws a dark blue point. The third call produces a lighter blue circle with sharp edges. The last call, `cv2.circle`, reveals the lightest blue circle with smooth borders.

The `cv2.circle` function takes the image as first parameter, and the position of center in (*x, y*) format, radius of the circle, and the color as mandatory arguments. Also you can specify line thickness (the `FILLED` value gives a filled circle) and line type (`LINE_AA` gives aliasing-free borders).

The `cv2.line` function takes an image, start and end points, and color of the image (as in first call). Optionally you can pass line thickness and line type (again, to suppress aliasing).

We will get something like this (positions may vary due to randomness):

The parameters of the cv2.arrowedLine function are the same as those for cv2.line.

The parameters that cv2.rectangle takes are the image that is to be drawn upon, the upper-left corner, bottom-right corner, and the color. Also, it's possible to specify thickness (or make the rectangle filled with the FILLED value).

cv2.ellipse takes the image, the position of the center in (x, y) format, half axis lengths in (a, b) format, the rotation angle, the start angle of drawing, the end angle of drawing, and color and thickness of line (you can also draw a filled ellipse) as parameters.

Arguments of the cv2.putText function are the image, the text being placed, the position of the bottom-left corner of the text, the name of the font face, the scale of symbols, and color and thickness.

Handling user input from a keyboard

OpenCV has simple and clear way to handle input from a keyboard. This functionality is organically built into the cv2.waitKey function. Let's see how we can use it.

Getting ready

You need to have OpenCV 3.x installed with Python API support.

How to do it...

You will need to perform the following steps for this recipe:

1. As done previously, open an image and get its width and height. Also, make a copy of the original image and define a simple function that returns a random point with coordinates inside our image:

```
import cv2, numpy as np, random

image = cv2.imread('../data/Lena.png')
w, h = image.shape[1], image.shape[0]
image_to_show = np.copy(image)

def rand_pt():
 return (random.randrange(w),
 random.randrange(h))
```

2. Now when the user presses *P, L, R, E,* or *T* draw points, lines, rectangles, ellipses, or text, respectively. Also, we will clear an image when the user hits *C* and closes the application when the *Esc* key is pushed:

```
finish = False
while not finish:
    cv2.imshow("result", image_to_show)
    key = cv2.waitKey(0)
    if key == ord('p'):
        for pt in [rand_pt() for _ in range(10)]:
            cv2.circle(image_to_show, pt, 3, (255, 0, 0), -1)
    elif key == ord('l'):
        cv2.line(image_to_show, rand_pt(), rand_pt(), (0, 255, 0),
3)
    elif key == ord('r'):
```

```
        cv2.rectangle(image_to_show, rand_pt(), rand_pt(), (0, 0,
255), 3)
    elif key == ord('e'):
        cv2.ellipse(image_to_show, rand_pt(), rand_pt(),
random.randrange(360), 0, 360, (255, 255, 0), 3)
    elif key == ord('t'):
        cv2.putText(image_to_show, 'OpenCV', rand_pt(),
cv2.FONT_HERSHEY_SIMPLEX, 1, (0, 0, 0), 3)
    elif key == ord('c'):
        image_to_show = np.copy(image)
    elif key == 27:
        finish = True
```

How it works...

As you can see, we just analyze the waitKey() return value. If we set a duration and no key is pressed, waitKey() would return -1.

After launching the code and pressing the *P, L, R, E,* and *T* keys a few times, you will get an image close to the following:

Making your app interactive through handling user input from a mouse

In this recipe, we will learn how to enable the handling of mouse input in your OpenCV application. An instance that gets events from a mouse is the window, so we need to use `cv2.imshow`. But we also need to add our handlers for mouse events. Let's see, in detail, how to do it by implementing crop functionality through selecting image regions by mouse.

Getting ready

You need to have OpenCV 3.x installed with Python API support.

How to do it...

The steps for this recipe are as follows:

1. First, load an image and make its copy:

```
import cv2, numpy as np

image = cv2.imread('../data/Lena.png')
image_to_show = np.copy(image)
```

2. Now, define some variables to store the mouse state:

```
mouse_pressed = False
s_x = s_y = e_x = e_y = -1
```

3. Let's implement a handler for mouse events. This should be a function that takes four arguments, as follows:

```
def mouse_callback(event, x, y, flags, param):
    global image_to_show, s_x, s_y, e_x, e_y, mouse_pressed

    if event == cv2.EVENT_LBUTTONDOWN:
        mouse_pressed = True
        s_x, s_y = x, y
        image_to_show = np.copy(image)

    elif event == cv2.EVENT_MOUSEMOVE:
        if mouse_pressed:
```

```
        image_to_show = np.copy(image)
        cv2.rectangle(image_to_show, (s_x, s_y),
                      (x, y), (0, 255, 0), 1)

    elif event == cv2.EVENT_LBUTTONUP:
        mouse_pressed = False
        e_x, e_y = x, y
```

4. Let's create the window instance that will be capturing mouse events and translating them into the handler function we defined earlier:

```
cv2.namedWindow('image')
cv2.setMouseCallback('image', mouse_callback)
```

5. Now, let's implement the remaining part of our application, which should be reacting to buttons pushes and cropping the original image:

```
while True:
    cv2.imshow('image', image_to_show)
    k = cv2.waitKey(1)

    if k == ord('c'):
        if s_y > e_y:
            s_y, e_y = e_y, s_y
        if s_x > e_x:
            s_x, e_x = e_x, s_x

        if e_y - s_y > 1 and e_x - s_x > 0:
            image = image[s_y:e_y, s_x:e_x]
            image_to_show = np.copy(image)
    elif k == 27:
        break

cv2.destroyAllWindows()
```

How it works...

In cv2.setMouseCallback, we assigned our mouse events handler, mouse_callback, to the window named image.

After launching, we will be able to select a region by pushing the left mouse button somewhere in the image, dragging the mouse to the end point, and releasing the mouse button to confirm that our selection is finished. We can repeat the process by clicking in a new place—the previous selection disappears:

By hitting the *C* button on the keyboard, we can cut an area inside the selected region, as follows:

Capturing and showing frames from a camera

In this recipe, you will learn how to connect to a USB camera and capture frames from it live using OpenCV.

Getting ready

You need to have OpenCV 3.x installed with Python API support.

How to do it...

For this recipe, the steps are as follows:

1. Create a `VideoCapture` object:

```
import cv2

capture = cv2.VideoCapture(0)
```

2. Read the frames from the camera using the `capture.read` method, which returns a pair: a read success flag and the `frame` itself:

```
while True:
    has_frame, frame = capture.read()
    if not has_frame:
        print('Can\'t get frame')
        break

    cv2.imshow('frame', frame)
    key = cv2.waitKey(3)
    if key == 27:
        print('Pressed Esc')
        break
```

3. It's generally recommended that you release the video device (a camera, in our case) and destroy all the windows created:

```
capture.release()
cv2.destroyAllWindows()
```

How it works...

Working with cameras in OpenCV is done through the `cv2.VideoCapture` class. In fact it provides support when working with both cameras and video files. To instantiate an object representing a frame stream coming from a camera, you should just specify its number (zero-based device index). If OpenCV doesn't support your camera out of the box, you can try recompiling OpenCV, turning on optional support of other industrial camera types.

Playing frame stream from video

In this recipe, you will learn how to open an existing video file using OpenCV. You will also learn how to replay frames from the opened video.

Getting ready

You need to have OpenCV 3.x installed with Python API support.

How to do it...

The following are the steps for this recipe:

1. Create a `VideoCapture` object for video file:

```
import cv2

capture = cv2.VideoCapture('../data/drop.avi')
```

2. Replay all the frames in the video:

```
while True:
    has_frame, frame = capture.read()
    if not has_frame:
        print('Reached the end of the video')
        break

    cv2.imshow('frame', frame)
    key = cv2.waitKey(50)
    if key == 27:
        print('Pressed Esc')
        break

cv2.destroyAllWindows()
```

How it works...

Working with video files is virtually the same as working with cameras—it's done through the same cv2.VideoCapture class. This time, however, instead of the camera device index, you should specify the path to the video file you want to open. Depending on the OS and video codecs available, OpenCV might not support some of the video formats.

After the video file is opened in a infinite while loop, we acquire frames using the capture.read method. The function returns a pair: a Boolean frame read success flag, and the frame itself. Note that frames are read at the maximum possible rate, meaning if you want to replay video at a certain FPS, you should implement it on your own. In the preceding code, after we call the cv2.imshow function, we wait for 50 milliseconds in the cv2.waitKey function. Assuming the time spent on showing the image and decoding the video is negligible, the video will be replayed at a rate no greater than 20 FPS.

The following frames are expected to be seen:

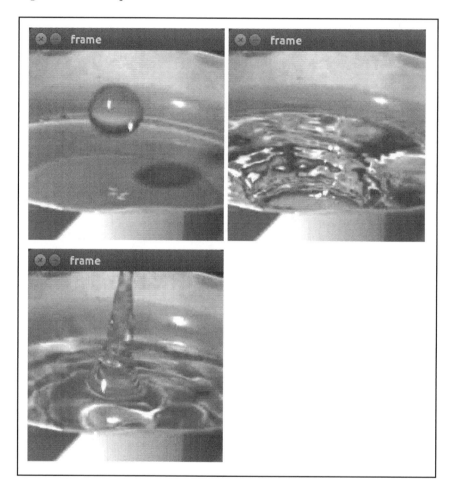

Obtaining a frame stream properties

In this recipe, you will learn how to get such VideoCapture properties as frame height and width, frame count for video files, and camera frame rate.

Getting ready

You need to have OpenCV 3.x installed with Python API support.

How to do it...

Execute the following steps:

1. Let's create an auxiliary function that will take the `VideoCapture` ID (either what the camera device is or the path to the video), create a `VideoCapture` object, and request the frame height and width, count, and rate:

```python
import numpy
import cv2

def print_capture_properties(*args):
    capture = cv2.VideoCapture(*args)
    print('Created capture:', ' '.join(map(str, args)))
    print('Frame count:',
int(capture.get(cv2.CAP_PROP_FRAME_COUNT)))
    print('Frame width:',
int(capture.get(cv2.CAP_PROP_FRAME_WIDTH)))
    print('Frame height:',
int(capture.get(cv2.CAP_PROP_FRAME_HEIGHT)))
    print('Frame rate:', capture.get(cv2.CAP_PROP_FPS))
```

2. Let's call this function for a video file:

```python
print_capture_properties('../data/drop.avi')
```

3. Now let's request properties for the camera capture object:

```python
print_capture_properties(0)
```

How it works...

As in the earlier recipes, working with cameras and video frame streams is done through the `cv2.VideoCapture` class. You can get properties using the `capture.get` function, which takes the property ID and returns its value as a floating-point value.

Note that, depending on the OS and video backend used, not all of the properties being requested can be accessed.

The following output is expected (it might vary depending on the OS and the video backend that OpenCV was compiled with):

```
Created capture: ../data/drop.avi
Frame count: 182
Frame width: 256
Frame height: 240
Frame rate: 30.0

Created capture: 0
Frame count: -1
Frame width: 640
Frame height: 480
Frame rate: 30.0
```

Writing a frame stream into video

In this recipe, you will learn how to capture frames from a USB camera live and simultaneously write frames into a video file using a specified video codec.

Getting ready

You need to have OpenCV 3.x installed with Python API support.

How to do it...

Here are the steps we need to execute in order to complete this recipe:

1. First, we create a camera capture object, as in the previous recipes, and get the frame height and width:

```
import cv2
capture = cv2.VideoCapture(0)
frame_width = int(capture.get(cv2.CAP_PROP_FRAME_WIDTH))
frame_height = int(capture.get(cv2.CAP_PROP_FRAME_HEIGHT))
print('Frame width:', frame_width)
print('Frame height:', frame_height)
```

2. Create a video writer:

```
video = cv2.VideoWriter('../data/captured_video.avi',
cv2.VideoWriter_fourcc(*'X264'),
                        25, (frame_width, frame_height))
```

3. Then, in an infinite `while` loop, capture frames and write them using the `video.write` method:

```
while True:
    has_frame, frame = capture.read()
    if not has_frame:
        print('Can\'t get frame')
        break
    video.write(frame)
    cv2.imshow('frame', frame)
    key = cv2.waitKey(3)
    if key == 27:
        print('Pressed Esc')
        break
```

4. Release all created `VideoCapture` and `VideoWriter` objects, and destroy the windows:

```
capture.release()
writer.release()
cv2.destroyAllWindows()
```

How it works...

Writing video is performed using the `cv2.VideoWriter` class. The constructor takes the output video path, **four characted code** (**FOURCC**) specifying video code, desired frame rate and frame size. Examples of codec codes include P, I, M, and 1 for MPEG-1; M, J, P, and G for motion-JPEG; X, V, I, and D for XVID MPEG-4; and H, 2, 6, and 4 for H.264.

Jumping between frames in video files

In this recipe, you will learn how to position `VideoCapture` objects at different frame positions.

Getting ready

You need to have OpenCV 3.x installed with Python API support.

How to do it...

The steps for this recipe are:

1. First, let's create a `VideoCapture` object and obtain the total number of frames:

```
import cv2
capture = cv2.VideoCapture('../data/drop.avi')
frame_count = int(capture.get(cv2.CAP_PROP_FRAME_COUNT))
print('Frame count:', frame_count)
```

2. Get the total number of frames:

```
print('Position:', int(capture.get(cv2.CAP_PROP_POS_FRAMES)))
_, frame = capture.read()
cv2.imshow('frame0', frame)
```

3. Note that the `capture.read` method advances the current video position one frame forward. Get the next frame:

```
print('Position:', capture.get(cv2.CAP_PROP_POS_FRAMES))
_, frame = capture.read()
cv2.imshow('frame1', frame)
```

4. Let's jump to frame position `100`:

```
capture.set(cv2.CAP_PROP_POS_FRAMES, 100)
print('Position:', int(capture.get(cv2.CAP_PROP_POS_FRAMES)))
_, frame = capture.read()
cv2.imshow('frame100', frame)

cv2.waitKey()
cv2.destroyAllWindows()
```

How it works...

Obtaining the video position and setting it is done using the `cv2.CAP_PROP_POS_FRAMES` property. Depending on the way a video is encoded, setting the property might not result in setting the exact frame index requested. The value to set must be within a valid range.

You should see the following output after running the program:

```
Frame count: 182
Position: 0
Position: 1
Position: 100
```

The following frames should be displayed:

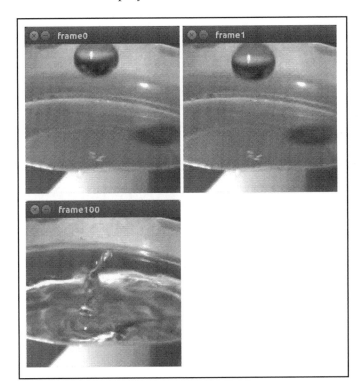

2
Matrices, Colors, and Filters

In this chapter, we will cover the following recipes:

- Manipulating matrices-creating, filling, accessing elements, and ROIs
- Converting between different data types and scaling values
- Non-image data persistence using NumPy
- Manipulating image channels
- Converting images from one color space to another
- Gamma correction and per-element math
- Mean/variance image normalization
- Computing image histograms
- Equalizing image histograms
- Removing noise using Gaussian, median, and bilateral filters
- Computing gradient images using Sobel filters
- Creating and applying your own filter
- Processing images with real-valued Gabor filters
- Going from the spatial to the frequency domain (and back) using discrete Fourier transform
- Manipulating image frequencies for image filtration
- Processing images with different thresholds
- Morphological operators
- Binary images-image masks and binary operations

Introduction

In this chapter, we will see how to work with matrices. We will learn what we can do with a matrix on a pixel level and what operations and image-processing procedures we can apply to the whole matrix. You will know how to get access to any pixel, how to change data types and color spaces of matrices, how to apply built-in OpenCV filters, and how to create and use your own linear filter.

Manipulating matrices-creating, filling, accessing elements, and ROIs

This recipe covers the creation and initialization of matrices, access to its elements, pixels, and also how we can work with part of a matrix.

Getting ready

You need to have OpenCV 3.x installed with Python API support.

How to do it...

To get the result, it's necessary to go through a few steps:

1. Import all necessary modules:

```
import cv2, numpy as np
```

2. Create a matrix of a certain shape and fill it with 255 as a value, which should display the following:

```
image = np.full((480, 640, 3), 255, np.uint8)
cv2.imshow('white', image)
cv2.waitKey()
cv2.destroyAllWindows()
```

3. Create a matrix and set individual values for the colors of each pixel to color our matrix red:

```
image = np.full((480, 640, 3), (0, 0, 255), np.uint8)
cv2.imshow('red', image)
cv2.waitKey()
cv2.destroyAllWindows()
```

4. Fill our matrix with zeros to make it black:

```
image.fill(0)
cv2.imshow('black', image)
cv2.waitKey()
cv2.destroyAllWindows()
```

5. Next, set some individual pixels' values to white:

```
image[240, 160] = image[240, 320] = image[240, 480] = (255, 255, 255)
cv2.imshow('black with white pixels', image)
cv2.waitKey()
cv2.destroyAllWindows()
```

6. Now, let's set the first channel of all pixels to 255 to make black ones blue:

```
image[:, :, 0] = 255
cv2.imshow('blue with white pixels', image)
cv2.waitKey()
cv2.destroyAllWindows()
```

7. Now, set pixels on a vertical line in the middle of the image to white:

```
image[:, 320, :] = 255
cv2.imshow('blue with white line', image)
cv2.waitKey()
cv2.destroyAllWindows()
```

8. Finally, set the second channel of all pixels inside a certain region to 255:

```
image[100:600, 100:200, 2] = 255
cv2.imshow('image', image)
cv2.waitKey()
cv2.destroyAllWindows()
```

How it works...

Matrices in OpenCV's Python interface are presented with NumPy arrays. NumPy provides powerful yet clear tools to deal with multi-dimensional matrices, which are also called tensors. And, of course, NumPy supports plain 2-dimensional matrices. That's why we need to import its module. And this is the reason why we're using a lot of np's functions in this recipe.

Here it's necessary to say a few words about matrix dimensions and types. Matrices have two independent characteristics—shape type and element type. Firstly, let's talk about shape. Shape describes all dimensions of the matrix. A matrix usually has three spatial dimensions: width (also called number of columns), height (also called number of rows), and number of channels. Usually it's subscribed in height, width, channels format. OpenCV works with full color or grayscale matrices. This means that only 3-channels or 1-channels may be handled by OpenCV routines. Grayscale matrices may be imagined as planar tables of numbers, where each element (pixel) stores only one value. Full color ones may be considered as tables where each element stores not one but three values in a row. An example of a full color matrix is one with red, green, and blue channels, respectively—this means each element stores values for red, green, and blue components. But for historical reasons, OpenCV stores color values for RGB representation in BGR format—so be careful.

Another feature of a matrix is its element type. The element type defines which data type is used to represent element values. For example, each pixel can store values in the [0-255] range—in this case, it is np.uint8. Or, it can store float (np.float32) or double (np.float64) values.

np.full is used to create matrices. It takes the following parameters: shape of the matrix in (height, width, channels) format, initial value for each pixel (or each component of the pixel), and the type of pixel value. It's possible to pass a single number as a second parameter—in this case, all pixel values are initialized with this number. Also, we can pass initial numbers for each pixel element.

np.fill helps you to assign the same values for all pixels—just pass a value to assign as a parameter. The difference here between np.fill and np.full is that the first one doesn't create a matrix but just assigns values to existing elements.

To get access to individual pixels, you can use the `[]` operator and specify indexes of the desired element; for example, `image[240, 160]` gives you access to the pixel at height `240` and width `160`. The order of the indexes corresponds with the order of dimensions in the matrix shape—the first index is along the first dimension, the second index is along the second dimension, and so on. If you specify indexes only for some dimensions, you'll get a slice (a tensor with a low dimension number). It's possible to address all the pixels along a dimension by using a colon (`:`) instead of index. For example, `image[:, 320, :]` actually means—*give all pixels along height and channels that have index 320 along the width dimension*.

The `:` symbol also helps to specify certain regions inside the matrix—we just need to add start the index before `:` and end the index after `:` (the end of an index isn't included in the range). For instance, `image[100:600, 100:200, 2]` gives us all pixels with height indexes in the range of `[100, 600]`, width indexes in the range of `[100, 200]`, and channel index `2`.

Converting between different data types and scaling values

This recipe tells you how to change the data type of matrix elements from `uint8` to `float32` and perform arithmetic operations without worrying about clamping values (and then convert everything back to `uint8`).

Getting ready

You need to have OpenCV 3.x installed with Python API support.

How to do it...

The following steps are required for this recipe:

1. Import all necessary modules, open an image, print its shape and data type, and display it on the screen:

```python
import cv2, numpy as np
image = cv2.imread('../data/Lena.png')
print('Shape:', image.shape)
print('Data type:', image.dtype)
```

```
cv2.imshow('image', image)
cv2.waitKey()
cv2.destroyAllWindows()
```

2. Convert our image to one with floating data type elements:

```
image = image.astype(np.float32) / 255
print('Shape:', image.shape)
print('Data type:', image.dtype)
```

3. Scale the elements of our image by 2 and clip the values to keep them in the [0, 1] range:

```
cv2.imshow('image', np.clip(image*2, 0, 1))
cv2.waitKey()
cv2.destroyAllWindows()
```

4. Scale the elements of our image back to the [0, 255] range, and convert the element type to 8-bit unsigned int:

```
image = (image * 255).astype(np.uint8)
print('Shape:', image.shape)
print('Data type:', image.dtype)

cv2.imshow('image', image)
cv2.waitKey()
cv2.destroyAllWindows()
```

How it works...

To convert the data type of the matrix, it's necessary to use the astype function of NumPy Array. The function takes desired type as input and returns converted array.

To scale the values of the matrix, you can use an algebraic operation with the matrix itself: for example, just divide the matrix by some value (255, in the preceding code) to divide each element of the matrix by the specified value. The result of scaling the values of the input images should appear as follows (the left image is the original, the right image is the scaled version):

Non-image data persistence using NumPy

Previously, we've saved and loaded only images with OpenCV's `cv2.imwrite` and `cv2.imread` functions, respectively. But it's possible to save any matrix (not only with image content) of any type and shape with NumPy's data persistence. In this recipe, we will review how to do it.

Getting ready

You need to have OpenCV 3.x installed with Python API support.

How to do it...

Perform the following steps:

1. Import all necessary modules:

   ```
   import cv2, numpy as np
   ```

2. Create a matrix with random values initialization and print its attributes:

   ```
   mat = np.random.rand(100, 100).astype(np.float32)
   print('Shape:', mat.shape)
   print('Data type:', mat.dtype)
   ```

3. Save our random matrix to the file with the `np.savetxt` function:

```
np.savetxt('mat.csv', mat)
```

4. Now, load it from the file we've just written and print its shape and type:

```
mat = np.loadtxt('mat.csv').astype(np.float32)
print('Shape:', mat.shape)
print('Data type:', mat.dtype)
```

How it works...

NumPy's `savetxt` and `loadtxt` functions let you store and load any matrices. They use text format, so you can view the content of the file in a text editor.

Manipulating image channels

This recipe is about dealing with matrix channels. Getting access to individual channels, swapping them, and performing algebraic operations are all covered here.

Getting ready

You need to have OpenCV 3.x installed with Python API support.

How to do it...

Perform the following steps:

1. Import all necessary modules, open the image, and output its shape:

```
import cv2, numpy as np
image = cv2.imread('../data/Lena.png').astype(np.float32) / 255
print('Shape:', image.shape)
```

2. Swap the red and blue channels and display the result:

```
image[:, :, [0, 2]] = image[:, :, [2, 0]]
cv2.imshow('blue_and_red_swapped', image)
```

```
cv2.waitKey()
cv2.destroyAllWindows()
```

3. Swap the channels back and scale them differently to change the colorization of the image:

```
image[:, :, [0, 2]] = image[:, :, [2, 0]]
image[:, :, 0] = (image[:, :, 0] * 0.9).clip(0, 1)
image[:, :, 1] = (image[:, :, 1] * 1.1).clip(0, 1)
cv2.imshow('image', image)
cv2.waitKey()
cv2.destroyAllWindows()
```

How it works...

The last dimension of the matrix is responsible for channels. That's why we're manipulating it in the code.

To swap channels, we should get access to the corresponding slices of our matrix. But slices aren't copies of the original matrix, they're just different views of the same data. This means we can't perform swaps through temporary variables as we do with plain types. We need something more complicated here, and NumPy allows us to get not only a single slice, but a bunch of slices as new views of the data. To do so, we should enumerate indexes for all needed slices in the desired order, instead of just a single index.

When we use a single index, we get an access to the corresponding channel, and we can perform some algebraic operations on the slice.

The results should appear as follows:

Converting images from one color space to another

This recipe tells you about color space conversion. By default, full color images in OpenCV are presented in RGB color space. But for some cases it's necessary to move to other color representations; for example, to have a separate channel for intensity. Here we consider ways to change the color space of an image.

Getting ready

You need to have OpenCV 3.x installed with Python API support.

How to do it...

Use following steps:

1. Import all necessary modules:

```
import cv2
import numpy as np
```

2. Load an image and print its shape and type:

```
image = cv2.imread('../data/Lena.png').astype(np.float32) / 255
print('Shape:', image.shape)
print('Data type:', image.dtype)
```

3. Convert the image to grayscale:

```
gray = cv2.cvtColor(image, cv2.COLOR_BGR2GRAY)
print('Converted to grayscale')
print('Shape:', gray.shape)
print('Data type:', gray.dtype)
cv2.imshow('gray', gray)
cv2.waitKey()
cv2.destroyAllWindows()
```

4. Convert the image to HSV color space:

```
hsv = cv2.cvtColor(image, cv2.COLOR_BGR2HSV)
print('Converted to HSV')
print('Shape:', hsv.shape)
print('Data type:', hsv.dtype)
cv2.imshow('hsv', hsv)
cv2.waitKey()
cv2.destroyAllWindows()
```

5. Increase the brightness of the image by multiplying the *V* channel by some value. Then convert the image to the RGB color space:

```
hsv[:, :, 2] *= 2
from_hsv = cv2.cvtColor(hsv, cv2.COLOR_HSV2BGR)
print('Converted back to BGR from HSV')
print('Shape:', from_hsv.shape)
print('Data type:', from_hsv.dtype)
cv2.imshow('from_hsv', from_hsv)
cv2.waitKey()
cv2.destroyAllWindows()
```

How it works...

To change the color space of an image with OpenCV, you should use the cvtColor function. It takes the source image and the special value, which encodes the source and targets the color spaces. The return value of the function is the converted image. OpenCV supports over 200 conversion types. The results of the code execution should be as follows:

Gamma correction and per-element math

Gamma correction is used to skew pixels, value distribution in a non-linear manner. With gamma correction, it's possible to adjust the luminescence of the image to make it easier to see. In this recipe, you will learn how to apply gamma correction to images.

Getting ready

You need to have OpenCV 3.x installed with Python API support.

How to do it...

The steps for this recipe are as follows:

1. Load the image as grayscale and convert every pixel value to the `np.float32` data type in the `[0, 1]` range:

```
import cv2
import numpy as np

image = cv2.imread('../data/Lena.png', 0).astype(np.float32) / 255
```

2. Apply per-element exponentiation using the specified exponent value, `gamma`:

```
gamma = 0.5
corrected_image = np.power(image, gamma)
```

3. Display the source and result images:

```
cv2.imshow('image', image)
cv2.imshow('corrected_image', corrected_image)
cv2.waitKey()
cv2.destroyAllWindows()
```

How it works...

Gamma correction is a non-linear operation that adjusts image pixel intensities. The operation is represented through the power-law relationship between input and output pixel values: $V_{out} = V_{in}^{\gamma}$. The values with an exponent coefficient higher than 1 make the image darker, while the values less than 1 make the image brighter.

The following output is expected for the preceding code:

Mean/variance image normalization

Sometimes it's necessary to set certain values to the statistical moments of pixel values. When we set 0 for mean value of values and 1 for variance, the operation is called normalization. This can be useful in computer vision algorithms for dealing with values with a certain range and with certain statistics. Here we're going to check out image normalization.

Getting ready

You need to have OpenCV 3.x installed with Python API support.

How to do it...

Perform the following steps:

1. Import all necessary modules:

```
import cv2
import numpy as np
```

2. Load an image and convert it to one with floating-point elements in range [0, 1]:

```
image = cv2.imread('../data/Lena.png').astype(np.float32) / 255
```

3. Subtract the mean value from each image pixel to get a zero-mean matrix. Then, divide each pixel value by its standard deviation to have a unit-variance matrix:

```
image -= image.mean()
image /= image.std()
```

How it works...

Matrices are presented with NumPy array classes. These arrays have methods to compute mean values and standard deviations. To normalize a matrix—that is, to get a zero-mean and unit-variance matrix—we need to subtract the mean value, which we can get by calling mean and dividing the matrix by its standard deviation. You can also use the cv2.meanStdDev function, which computes both mean and standard deviation simultaneously.

Computing image histograms

Histograms show the levels distribution in a set of values; for example, in an image. In this recipe, we understand how to compute histograms.

Getting ready

You need to have OpenCV 3.x installed with Python API support.

How to do it...

Follow these steps:

1. Import all necessary modules:

    ```
    import cv2
    import numpy as np
    import matplotlib.pyplot as plt
    ```

2. Load an image and display it:

    ```
    grey = cv2.imread('../data/Lena.png', 0)
    cv2.imshow('original grey', grey)
    cv2.waitKey()
    cv2.destroyAllWindows()
    ```

3. Compute a `histogram` function:

    ```
    hist, bins = np.histogram(grey, 256, [0, 255])
    ```

4. Plot `histogram` and display it:

    ```
    plt.fill(hist)
    plt.xlabel('pixel value')
    plt.show()
    ```

How it works...

OpenCV has its own generic function for computing histograms, `cv2.calcHist`. However, in this recipe, we will use NumPy since, in this particular case, it makes code more concise. NumPy has a special function to compute histograms, `np.histogram`. Arguments of the routine are the input image, number of bins, and range of bins. It returns an array with histogram values and edge values for bins.

To plot the histogram as a figure, we need to use functionality from the matplotlib module. The output figure should appear as follows:

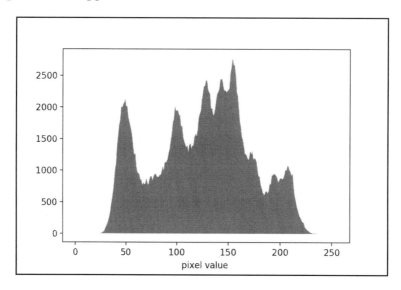

Equalizing image histograms

Image histograms are used to reflect intensity distribution. Properties of histograms depend on image properties. For example, low-contrast images have histograms where bins are clustered near a value: most of the pixels have their values within a narrow range. Low-contrast images are harder to work with because small details are poorly expressed. There is a technique that is able to address this issue. It's called histogram equalization. This recipe covers usage of the approach in OpenCV. We study how to perform histogram equalization for both grayscale and full color images.

Getting ready

You need to have OpenCV 3.x installed with Python API support.

How to do it...

Use the following steps:

1. Import all necessary modules:

```
import cv2
import numpy as np
import matplotlib.pyplot as plt
```

2. Load the image as grayscale and display it:

```
grey = cv2.imread('../data/Lena.png', 0)
cv2.imshow('original grey', grey)
cv2.waitKey()
cv2.destroyAllWindows()
```

3. Equalize the histogram of the grayscale image:

```
grey_eq = cv2.equalizeHist(grey)
```

4. Compute the histogram for the equalized image and show it:

```
hist, bins = np.histogram(grey_eq, 256, [0, 255])
plt.fill_between(range(256), hist, 0)
plt.xlabel('pixel value')
plt.show()
```

5. Show the equalized image:

```
cv2.imshow('equalized grey', grey_eq)
cv2.waitKey()
cv2.destroyAllWindows()
```

6. Load the image as BGR and convert it to the HSV color space:

```
color = cv2.imread('../data/Lena.png')
hsv = cv2.cvtColor(color, cv2.COLOR_BGR2HSV)
```

7. Equalize the *V* channel of the HSV image and convert it back to the RGB color space:

```
hsv[..., 2] = cv2.equalizeHist(hsv[..., 2])
color_eq = cv2.cvtColor(hsv, cv2.COLOR_HSV2BGR)
cv2.imshow('original color', color)
```

8. Show the equalized full color image:

```
cv2.imshow('equalized color', color_eq)
cv2.waitKey()
cv2.destroyAllWindows()
```

How it works...

To equalize histograms, a special function from OpenCV can be applied. It's called `equalizeHist`, and it takes an image whose contrast we need to be enhanced. Note that it takes only single-channel images, so we can use this function directly only for grayscale images. The return value of the routine is a single-channel, equalized image.

To apply this function for full color images, we need to transform them in such way as to have intensity information in one channel and color information in the other channels. The HSV color space perfectly fits this requirement, because the last *V* channel encodes brightness. By transforming an input image to HSV color space, applying `equalizeHist` to the *V* channel, and converting the result back to RGB, we can equalize histogram for full color images.

After following the steps from this recipe, the result should appear as follows:

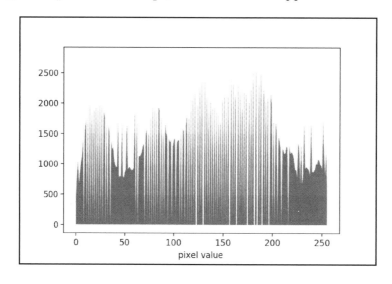

Removing noise using Gaussian, median, and bilateral filters

All real images are noisy. Noise not only spoils the appearance of the image but also it makes harder for your algorithms to handle them as input. In this recipe, we consider how to get rid of noise or dramatically decrease it.

Getting ready

Install the OpenCV 3.x Python API package and the `matplotlib` package.

How to do it...

Perform the following steps:

1. Import the packages:

```
import cv2
import numpy as np
import matplotlib.pyplot as plt
```

2. Load an image, convert it to floating-point, and scale it down to the `[0, 1]` range:

```
image = cv2.imread('../data/Lena.png').astype(np.float32) / 255
```

3. Create noise in the image by adding random values to each pixel, and display it:

```
noised = (image + 0.2 *
np.random.rand(*image.shape).astype(np.float32))
noised = noised.clip(0, 1)
plt.imshow(noised[:,:,[2,1,0]])
plt.show()
```

4. Apply `GaussianBlur` to the noisy image and show the result:

```
gauss_blur = cv2.GaussianBlur(noised, (7, 7), 0)
plt.imshow(gauss_blur[:, :, [2, 1, 0]])
plt.show()
```

5. Apply `median` filtering:

```
median_blur = cv2.medianBlur((noised * 255).astype(np.uint8), 7)
plt.imshow(median_blur[:, :, [2, 1, 0]])
plt.show()
```

6. Perform `median` filtration to our image with noise:

```
bilat = cv2.bilateralFilter(noised, -1, 0.3, 10)
plt.imshow(bilat[:, :, [2, 1, 0]])
plt.show()
```

How it works...

`cv2.GaussianBlur` is used to apply a `Gaussian` filter to the image. This function takes an input image, kernel size in (kernel width, kernel height) format, and standard deviations along width and height. The kernel size should be a positive, odd number.

If the standard deviation along height isn't specified or is set to zero, the value of X standard deviation is used for both directions. Also standard deviations can be computed from kernel sizes if we change X standard deviation to zero.

To apply `median` blurring, you need to use the `cv2.medianBlur` function. It accepts an input image as the first argument, and a kernel size as the second. Kernel size must be a positive, odd number.

Bilateral filtering is presented with the `cv2.bilateralFilter` function. It takes an input image, window size and color, and spatial sigma values. If the window size is negative, it's computed from spatial sigma values.

The various outputs of the preceding codes should appear as follows:

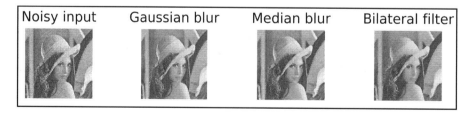

Computing gradients using Sobel operator

In this recipe, you will learn how to compute the approximation of an image's gradient using `Sobel` filters.

Getting ready

Install the OpenCV 3.x Python API package and the `matplotlib` package.

How to do it...

Perform the following steps:

1. Import the packages:

```
import cv2
import numpy as np
import matplotlib.pyplot as plt
```

2. Read the image as grayscale:

```
image = cv2.imread('../data/Lena.png', 0)
```

3. Compute the gradient approximations using the `Sobel` operator:

```
dx = cv2.Sobel(image, cv2.CV_32F, 1, 0)
dy = cv2.Sobel(image, cv2.CV_32F, 0, 1)
```

4. Visualize the results:

```
plt.figure(figsize=(8,3))
plt.subplot(131)
plt.axis('off')
plt.title('image')
plt.imshow(image, cmap='gray')
plt.subplot(132)
plt.axis('off')
plt.imshow(dx, cmap='gray')
plt.title(r'$\frac{dI}{dx}$')
plt.subplot(133)
plt.axis('off')
plt.title(r'$\frac{dI}{dy}$')
plt.imshow(dy, cmap='gray')
```

```
plt.tight_layout()
plt.show()
```

How it works...

OpenCV's `cv2.Sobel` function computes image gradient approximation using a linear filter of a specified size. Through function parameters, you can specify exactly what derivative needs to be computed, what kernel should be used, and the datatype for the output image.

The following output is expected for the preceding code:

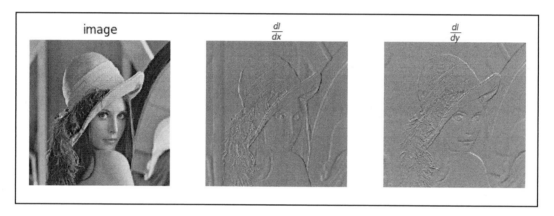

Creating and applying your own filter

In this recipe, you will learn how to create your own linear filter and apply it to images.

Getting ready

Install the OpenCV 3.x Python API package and the `matplotlib` package.

How to do it...

Perform the following steps:

1. Import the packages:

```
import math
import cv2
import numpy as np
import matplotlib.pyplot as plt
```

2. Read the test image:

```
image = cv2.imread('../data/Lena.png')
```

3. Create an 11x11 sharpening kernel:

```
KSIZE = 11
ALPHA = 2

kernel = cv2.getGaussianKernel(KSIZE, 0)
kernel = -ALPHA * kernel @ kernel.T
kernel[KSIZE//2, KSIZE//2] += 1 + ALPHA
```

4. Filter the image using the kernel we just created:

```
filtered = cv2.filter2D(image, -1, kernel)
```

5. Visualize the results:

```
plt.figure(figsize=(8,4))
plt.subplot(121)
plt.axis('off')
plt.title('image')
plt.imshow(image[:, :, [2, 1, 0]])
plt.subplot(122)
plt.axis('off')
plt.title('filtered')
plt.imshow(filtered[:, :, [2, 1, 0]])
plt.tight_layout(True)
plt.show()
```

How it works...

OpenCV's `cv2.filter2d` function takes an input image, output result datatype, OpenCV ID (-1, if you want to keep the input image datatype), and filter kernel; then, image is filtered linearly.

In this recipe, we constructed a sharpening kernel that should emphasize high frequencies in the source image. The following output is expected:

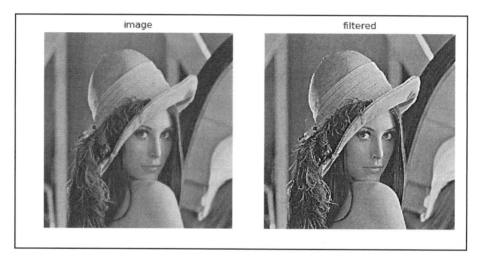

Processing images with real-valued Gabor filters

In this recipe, you will learn how to construct a `Gabor` filter kernel (useful for detecting edges in images) and apply it to an image.

Getting ready

Install the OpenCV 3.x Python API package and the `matplotlib` package.

How to do it...

Perform the following steps:

1. Import the packages:

```
import math
import cv2
import numpy as np
import matplotlib.pyplot as plt
```

2. Read the test image as grayscale and convert it to `np.float32`:

```
image = cv2.imread('../data/Lena.png', 0).astype(np.float32) / 255
```

3. Construct the real-valued `Gabor` filter kernel. Normalize the kernel in such a way that it has an L2 unit norm:

```
kernel = cv2.getGaborKernel((21, 21), 5, 1, 10, 1, 0, cv2.CV_32F)
kernel /= math.sqrt((kernel * kernel).sum())
```

4. Filter the image:

```
filtered = cv2.filter2D(image, -1, kernel)
```

5. Visualize the results:

```
plt.figure(figsize=(8,3))
plt.subplot(131)
plt.axis('off')
plt.title('image')
plt.imshow(image, cmap='gray')
plt.subplot(132)
plt.title('kernel')
plt.imshow(kernel, cmap='gray')
plt.subplot(133)
plt.axis('off')
plt.title('filtered')
plt.imshow(filtered, cmap='gray')
plt.tight_layout()
plt.show()
```

How it works...

The `Gabor` filter is a linear filter whose kernel is a 2D Gaussian modulated with a cosine wave. The kernel can be obtained using the `cv2.getGaborKernel` function, which takes such parameters as kernel size, Gaussian standard deviation, wave orientation, wave length, spatial ratio, and phase. One of the areas where `Gabor` filters are useful is detecting edges of known orientation.

The following output is expected:

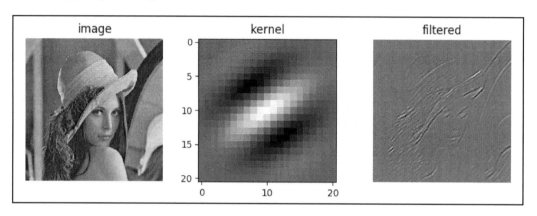

Going from the spatial domain to the frequency domain (and back) using the discrete Fourier transform

In this recipe, you will learn how to convert a grayscale image from spatial representation to frequency representation, and back again, using the discrete Fourier transform.

Getting ready

Install the OpenCV 3.x Python package and the `matplotlib` package.

How to do it...

The following steps must be performed:

1. Import the required packages:

```
import cv2
import numpy as np
import matplotlib.pyplot as plt
```

2. Read the image as grayscale and convert it to `np.float32` datatype:

```
image = cv2.imread('../data/Lena.png', 0).astype(np.float32) / 255
```

3. Apply the discrete Fourier transform:

```
fft = cv2.dft(image, flags=cv2.DFT_COMPLEX_OUTPUT)
```

4. Visualize image spectrum:

```
shifted = np.fft.fftshift(fft, axes=[0, 1])
magnitude = cv2.magnitude(shifted[:, :, 0], shifted[:, :, 1])
magnitude = np.log(magnitude)

plt.axis('off')
plt.imshow(magnitude, cmap='gray')
plt.tight_layout()
plt.show()
```

5. Convert the image from the frequency spectrum back to spatial representation:

```
restored = cv2.idft(fft, flags=cv2.DFT_SCALE | cv2.DFT_REAL_OUTPUT)
```

How it works...

OpenCV uses a fast Fourier transform algorithm (it's implemented by the `cv2.dft` function) for computing the discrete Fourier transform, and uses the same for its inverse version (the `cv2.idft` function). The functions support optional flags specifying whether output should be real or complex (flags `cv2.DFT_REAL_OUTPUT` and `cv2.DFT_COMPLEX_OUTPUT`, respectively), and whether output values should be scaled (using the `cv2.DFT_SCALE` flag). The `np.fft.fftshift` function shifts the frequency spectrum in such a way that the amplitude corresponding to zero frequency becomes located at the center of the array, and it's easier to interpret and work with further.

The following output is expected:

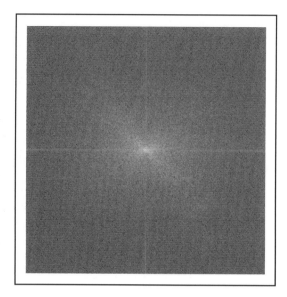

Manipulating image frequencies for image filtration

In this recipe, you will learn how to manipulate images in the frequency domain.

Getting ready

Install the OpenCV 3.x Python API package and the `matplotlib` package.

How to do it...

Perform the following steps:

1. Import the packages:

```
import cv2
import numpy as np
import matplotlib.pyplot as plt
```

2. Read the image as grayscale and convert it to the `np.float32` datatype:

```
image = cv2.imread('../data/Lena.png', 0).astype(np.float32) / 255
```

3. Convert the image from the spatial domain to the frequency domain using the discrete Fourier transform:

```
fft = cv2.dft(image, flags=cv2.DFT_COMPLEX_OUTPUT)
```

4. Shift the FFT results in such a way that low frequencies are located at the center of the array:

```
fft_shift = np.fft.fftshift(fft, axes=[0, 1])
```

5. Set the amplitudes for high frequencies to zero, leaving the others untouched:

```
sz = 25
mask = np.zeros(fft_shift.shape, np.uint8)
mask[mask.shape[0]//2-sz:mask.shape[0]//2+sz,
    mask.shape[1]//2-sz:mask.shape[1]//2+sz, :] = 1
fft_shift *= mask
```

6. Shift the DFT results back:

```
fft = np.fft.ifftshift(fft_shift, axes=[0, 1])
```

7. Convert the filtered image from the frequency domain back to the spatial domain using the inverse discrete Fourier transform:

```
filtered = cv2.idft(fft, flags=cv2.DFT_SCALE | cv2.DFT_REAL_OUTPUT)
```

8. Visualize the original and filtered images:

```
plt.figure()
plt.subplot(121)
plt.axis('off')
plt.title('original')
plt.imshow(image, cmap='gray')
plt.subplot(122)
plt.axis('off')
plt.title('no high frequencies')
plt.imshow(filtered, cmap='gray')
plt.tight_layout()
plt.show()
```

How it works...

Using fast Fourier transform, we convert the image from the spatial domain to the frequency domain. Then, we create a mask with zeros everywhere except a rectangle at the center. Using that mask, we set amplitudes for high frequencies to zero and convert the image back to spatial representation.

The following output is expected:

 For readers interested in more applications of the frequency domain filtering technique, we refer you to *Chapter 6, Seeing a Heartbeat with a Motion Amplifying Camera* of the book *OpenCV for Secret Agents* (https://www.packtpub.com/application-development/opencv-secret-agents).

Processing images with different thresholds

In this recipe, you will learn how to convert a grayscale image into a binary image using different thresholding approaches.

Getting ready

Install the OpenCV 3.x Python API package and the `matplotlib` package.

How to do it...

Perform the following steps:

1. Import the packages:

```
import cv2
import numpy as np
import matplotlib.pyplot as plt
```

2. Read the test image:

```
image = cv2.imread('../data/Lena.png', 0)
```

3. Apply a simple binary threshold:

```
thr, mask = cv2.threshold(image, 200, 1, cv2.THRESH_BINARY)
print('Threshold used:', thr)
```

4. Apply adaptive thresholding:

```
adapt_mask = cv2.adaptiveThreshold(image, 255,
cv2.ADAPTIVE_THRESH_MEAN_C,
                    cv2.THRESH_BINARY_INV, 11, 10)
```

5. Visualize the results:

```
plt.figure(figsize=(10,3))
plt.subplot(131)
plt.axis('off')
plt.title('original')
plt.imshow(image, cmap='gray')
plt.subplot(132)
plt.axis('off')
```

```
plt.title('binary threshold')
plt.imshow(mask, cmap='gray')
plt.subplot(133)
plt.axis('off')
plt.title('adaptive threshold')
plt.imshow(adapt_mask, cmap='gray')
plt.tight_layout()
plt.show()
```

How it works...

OpenCV has many different types of thresholds and thresholding methods. You can divide all the methods into two groups—global, where the same threshold value is used for all pixels, and adaptive, where the value of the threshold is pixel-dependent.

The approaches from the first group can be used through the cv2.threshold function, which, among other parameters, takes the threshold type (such as cv2.THRESH_BINARY and cv.THRESH_BINARY_INV).

Adaptive thresholding methods are available through the cv2.adaptiveThreshold function. In adaptive approaches, each pixel has its own threshold, which depends on the surrounding pixel values. In the preceding code, we used the cv2.ADAPTIVE_THRESH_MEAN_C approach for threshold value estimation, which computes the mean value of the surrounding pixels and uses that value minus a user-specified bias (10, in our case) as a pixel-wise threshold.

The various outputs for the preceding code should appear as follows:

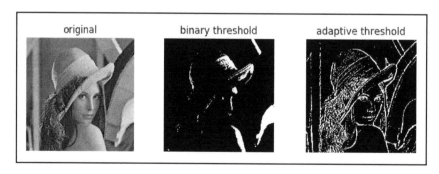

Morphological operators

In this recipe, you will learn how to apply basic morphological operations to binary images.

Getting ready

Install the OpenCV Python API package and the `matplotlib` package.

How to do it...

Follow these steps:

1. Import the packages:

    ```
    import cv2
    import numpy as np
    import matplotlib.pyplot as plt
    ```

2. Read the test image and build a binary image using Otsu's method:

    ```
    image = cv2.imread('../data/Lena.png', 0)
    _, binary = cv2.threshold(image, -1, 1, cv2.THRESH_BINARY |
    cv2.THRESH_OTSU)
    ```

3. Apply erosion and dilatation 10 times using a 3x3 rectangle mask:

    ```
    eroded = cv2.morphologyEx(binary, cv2.MORPH_ERODE, (3, 3),
    iterations=10)
    dilated = cv2.morphologyEx(binary, cv2.MORPH_DILATE, (3, 3),
    iterations=10)
    ```

4. Apply morphological open and close operations using an ellipse-like 5x5
    structuring element 5 times:

    ```
    opened = cv2.morphologyEx(binary, cv2.MORPH_OPEN,
    cv2.getStructuringElement(cv2.MORPH_ELLIPSE, (5, 5)),
                              iterations=5)
    closed = cv2.morphologyEx(binary, cv2.MORPH_CLOSE,
    cv2.getStructuringElement(cv2.MORPH_ELLIPSE, (5, 5)),
                              iterations=5)
    ```

5. Compute the morphological gradient:

```
grad = cv2.morphologyEx(binary, cv2.MORPH_GRADIENT,
cv2.getStructuringElement(cv2.MORPH_ELLIPSE, (5, 5)))
```

6. Visualize the results:

```
plt.figure(figsize=(10,10))
plt.subplot(231)
plt.axis('off')
plt.title('binary')
plt.imshow(binary, cmap='gray')
plt.subplot(232)
plt.axis('off')
plt.title('erode 10 times')
plt.imshow(eroded, cmap='gray')
plt.subplot(233)
plt.axis('off')
plt.title('dilate 10 times')
plt.imshow(dilated, cmap='gray')
plt.subplot(234)
plt.axis('off')
plt.title('open 5 times')
plt.imshow(opened, cmap='gray')
plt.subplot(235)
plt.axis('off')
plt.title('close 5 times')
plt.imshow(closed, cmap='gray')
plt.subplot(236)
plt.axis('off')
plt.title('gradient')
plt.imshow(grad, cmap='gray')
plt.tight_layout()
plt.show()
```

How it works...

The following output is expected:

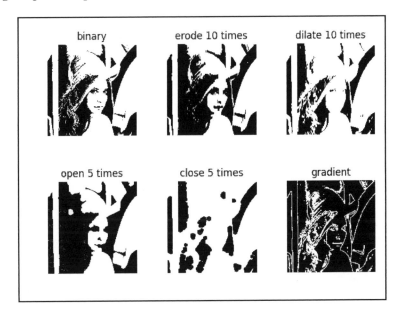

Image masks and binary operations

In this recipe, you will learn how to work with binary images, including how to apply binary element-wise operations.

Getting ready

You need to have OpenCV 3.x installed with Python API support and, additionally, the matplotlib package.

How to do it...

The steps for this recipe are as follows:

1. Import all the packages:

```
import cv2
import numpy as np
import matplotlib.pyplot as plt
```

2. Create a binary image with a circle mask:

```
circle_image = np.zeros((500, 500), np.uint8)
cv2.circle(circle_image, (250, 250), 100, 255, -1)
```

3. Create a binary image with a rectangle mask:

```
rect_image = np.zeros((500, 500), np.uint8)
cv2.rectangle(rect_image, (100, 100), (400, 250), 255, -1)
```

4. Combine the circle and rectangle masks using a bitwise AND operator:

```
circle_and_rect_image = circle_image & rect_image
```

5. Combine the circle and rectangle masks using a bitwise OR operator:

```
circle_or_rect_image = circle_image | rect_image
```

6. Visualize the results:

```
plt.figure(figsize=(10,10))
plt.subplot(221)
plt.axis('off')
plt.title('circle')
plt.imshow(circle_image, cmap='gray')
plt.subplot(222)
plt.axis('off')
plt.title('rectangle')
plt.imshow(rect_image, cmap='gray')
plt.subplot(223)
plt.axis('off')
plt.title('circle & rectangle')
plt.imshow(circle_and_rect_image, cmap='gray')
plt.subplot(224)
plt.axis('off')
plt.title('circle | rectangle')
plt.imshow(circle_or_rect_image, cmap='gray')
```

```
plt.tight_layout()
plt.show()
```

How it works...

It's convenient to represent binary images—images containing only black and white pixels—using `np.uint8` arrays with only `0` and `255` values correspondingly. Both OpenCV and NumPy support all usual binary operators: NOT, AND, OR, and XOR. They are available through aliases, such as ~, &, |, ^, as well as through functions such as `cv2.bitwise_not/np.bitwise_not` and `cv2.bitwise_and/np.bitwise_and`.

After running the preceding code, the following output is expected:

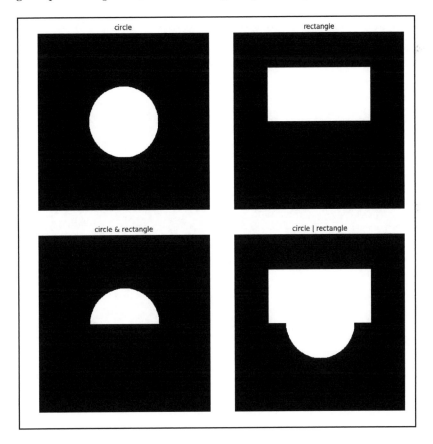

3
Contours and Segmentation

In this chapter, we will cover the following recipes:

- Binarization of grayscale images using the Otsu algorithm
- Finding external and internal contours in a binary image
- Extracting connected components from a binary image
- Fitting lines and circles into two-dimensional point sets
- Calculating image moments
- Working with curves - approximation, length, and area
- Checking whether a point is within a contour
- Computing the distance to a two-dimensional point set from every pixel
- Image segmentation using the k-means algorithm
- Image segmentation using segment seeds, the watershed algorithm

Introduction

Pixels store values. Values themselves are good features of an image—they can tell you about image statistics, but almost nothing more. Values group together according to image content—dark to light transitions form borders, and borders divide scenes into different objects. Borders connect together and reveal contours. Contours play an important role in many computer vision algorithms. They help to find objects, to separate one instance of something from another, and finally, to understand the whole scene.

This chapter sheds light on everything relevant to the contours in OpenCV. We will discuss methods for finding, using, and displaying them, as well as consider basic segmentation methods.

Binarization of grayscale images using the Otsu algorithm

Converting grayscale images to binary images using Otsu's method is useful when you have only two classes in an input image and want to extract them without any manual threshold adjusting. In this recipe, you will learn how to do it.

Getting ready

Before you proceed with this recipe, you will need to install the OpenCV 3.x Python API package and the `matplotlib` package.

How to do it...

To complete this recipe, we need to perform the following steps:

1. Import the modules:

```
import cv2
import numpy as np
import matplotlib.pyplot as plt
```

2. Read the test image:

```
image = cv2.imread('../data/Lena.png', 0)
```

3. Estimate the threshold using Otsu's method:

```
otsu_thr, otsu_mask = cv2.threshold(image, -1, 1, cv2.THRESH_BINARY
| cv2.THRESH_OTSU)
print('Estimated threshold (Otsu):', otsu_thr)
```

4. Visualize the results:

```
plt.figure()
plt.subplot(121)
plt.axis('off')
plt.title('original')
plt.imshow(image, cmap='gray')
plt.subplot(122)
plt.axis('off')
```

```
plt.title('Otsu threshold')
plt.imshow(otsu_mask, cmap='gray')
plt.tight_layout()
plt.show()
```

How it works...

Otsu's method estimates the threshold for grayscale images in such a way that after binarization and converting the original image to a binary mask, the total intra-class variance for two classes is minimal. Otsu's method can be used with the help of the `cv2.threshold` function, having specified the flag `cv2.THRESH_OTSU`.

The following output is expected from the preceding code:

```
Estimated threshold (Otsu): 116.0
```

Finding external and internal contours in a binary image

Having contours extracted from a binary image gives you an alternative image representation and allows you to apply contour-specific image analysis methods. In this recipe, you will learn how to find contours in a binary image.

Getting ready

For this recipe, ensure that you have installed the OpenCV 3.x Python API package and the `matplotlib` package.

How to do it...

1. Import the modules:

```
import cv2
import numpy as np
import matplotlib.pyplot as plt
```

2. Load the test binary image:

```
image = cv2.imread('../data/BnW.png', 0)
```

3. Find the external and internal contours. Organize them into a two-level hierarchy:

```
_, contours, hierarchy = cv2.findContours(image, cv2.RETR_CCOMP,
cv2.CHAIN_APPROX_SIMPLE)
```

4. Prepare the external contour binary mask:

```
image_external = np.zeros(image.shape, image.dtype)
for i in range(len(contours)):
    if hierarchy[0][i][3] == -1:
        cv2.drawContours(image_external, contours, i,
        255, -1)
```

5. Prepare the internal contour binary mask:

```
image_internal = np.zeros(image.shape, image.dtype)
for i in range(len(contours)):
    if hierarchy[0][i][3] != -1:
        cv2.drawContours(image_internal, contours, i,
        255, -1)
```

6. Visualize the results:

```
plt.figure(figsize=(10,3))
plt.subplot(131)
plt.axis('off')
plt.title('original')
plt.imshow(image, cmap='gray')
plt.subplot(132)
plt.axis('off')
plt.title('external')
plt.imshow(image_external, cmap='gray')
plt.subplot(133)
plt.axis('off')
plt.title('internal')
plt.imshow(image_internal, cmap='gray')
plt.tight_layout()
plt.show()
```

How it works...

Contours are extracted using the OpenCV function `cv2.findContours`. It supports different contour extraction modes:

- `cv2.RETR_EXTERNAL`: For extracting only external contours
- `cv2.RETR_CCOMP`: For extracting both internal and external contours, and organizing them into a two-level hierarchy
- `cv2.RETR_TREE`: For extracting both internal and external contours, and organizing them into a tree graph
- `cv2.RETR_LIST`: For extracting all contours without establishing any relationships

Also, you can specify whether contour compression is required (use `cv2.CHAIN_APPROX_SIMPLE` for collapsing vertical and horizontal parts of contours into their respective end points) or not (`cv2.CHAIN_APPROX_NONE`).

The function returns a tuple of three elements, modified image, list of contours, and list of contour hierarchy attributes. The hierarchy attributes describe the image contour topology, each list element is a four-element tuple containing zero-based indices of the next and previous contours at the same hierarchy level, then the first child and the first parent contours, respectively. If there's no contour, the corresponding index is -1.

The following output is expected:

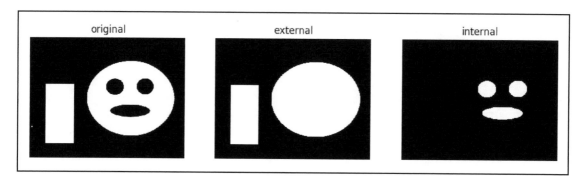

Extracting connected components from a binary image

Connected components in binary images are areas of non-zero values. Each element of each connected component is surrounded by at least one other element from the same component. And different components don't touch each other, there are zeros around each one.

Connected component analysis can be an important part of image processing. Typically (and in OpenCV, it's a fact), finding connected components in an image is much faster than finding all contours. So, it's possible to quickly exclude all irrelevant parts of the image according to connected component features (such as area, centroid location, and so on), to continue working with, remaining areas.

This recipe shows you how to find connected components on binary images with OpenCV.

Getting ready

You need to have OpenCV 3.x installed, with Python API support.

How to do it...

In order to execute this recipe, we will perform the following steps:

1. First, we import all of the modules we need:

   ```
   import cv2
   import numpy as np
   ```

2. Open an image and find the connected components in it:

   ```
   img = cv2.imread('../data/BnW.png', cv2.IMREAD_GRAYSCALE)

   connectivity = 8
   num_labels, labelmap = cv2.connectedComponents(img, connectivity,
   cv2.CV_32S)
   ```

3. Show the original image with the scaled image with labels:

   ```
   img = np.hstack((img, labelmap.astype(np.float32)/(num_labels -
   1)))
   cv2.imshow('Connected components', img)
   cv2.waitKey()
   cv2.destroyAllWindows()
   ```

4. Open another image, find its Otsu mask, and get the connected components with their statistics:

   ```
   img = cv2.imread('../data/Lena.png', cv2.IMREAD_GRAYSCALE)
   otsu_thr, otsu_mask = cv2.threshold(img, -1, 1, cv2.THRESH_BINARY |
   cv2.THRESH_OTSU)

   output = cv2.connectedComponentsWithStats(otsu_mask, connectivity,
   cv2.CV_32S)
   ```

5. Filter out the components with small areas and create a color image, upon which to draw the remaining components with individual colors, as well as the center of each component. Then, display the result:

   ```
   num_labels, labelmap, stats, centers = output

   colored = np.full((img.shape[0], img.shape[1], 3), 0, np.uint8)

   for l in range(1, num_labels):
       if stats[l][4] > 200:
           colored[labelmap == l] = (0, 255*l/num_labels,
   ```

```
255*num_labels/l)
        cv2.circle(colored,
                    (int(centers[l][0]), int(centers[l][1])), 5,
(255, 0, 0), cv2.FILLED)
img = cv2.cvtColor(otsu_mask*255, cv2.COLOR_GRAY2BGR)

cv2.imshow('Connected components', np.hstack((img, colored)))
cv2.waitKey()
cv2.destroyAllWindows()
```

How it works...

There are two functions in OpenCV that can be used to find connected components: `cv2.connectedComponents` and `cv2.connectedComponentsWithStats`. Both take the same arguments: the binary image whose components are to be found, the connectivity type, and the depth of the output image, with labels for components. Return values will vary.

`cv2.connectedComponents` is simpler, and returns a tuple of component numbers and an image with labels for components (`labelmap`). In addition to the previous function's outputs, `cv2.connectedComponentsWithStats` also returns statistics about each component and the components' centroid locations.

The labelmap has the same size as the input image, and each of its pixels has a value in the range [0, components number], according to which component the pixel belongs to. Statistics are represented by a Numpy array of the shape (components number, 5). The five elements correspond to the (*x0*, *y0*, width, height, area) structure. The first four elements are parameters of the bounding box for the component elements, and the last parameter is the area of the corresponding connected component. The centroids' locations are also Numpy arrays, but with the shape (components number, 2) where each row represents the (*x*, *y*) coordinates of the component's center.

After executing the code, you will get an image similar to the following:

Fitting lines and circles into two-dimensional point sets

Many computer vision algorithms deal with points. They may be contour points, or key points, or something else. And, in some cases, we know that all of these points should lie on the same curve, with a known mathematical shape. The process of finding the parameters of the curve (in the case of noisy data) is called approximation. Here, we're going to review two functions from OpenCV which find approximations for the ellipse and line for a set of points.

Getting ready

You need to have OpenCV 3.x installed, with Python API support.

How to do it...

1. First, import all of the modules:

```
import cv2
import numpy as np
import random
```

2. Create an image where we're going to draw and randomly generate parameters of the ellipse, such as half axes lengths and rotation angle:

```
img = np.full((512, 512, 3), 255, np.uint8)

axes = (int(256*random.uniform(0, 1)), int(256*random.uniform(0,
1)))
angle = int(180*random.uniform(0, 1))
center = (256, 256)
```

3. Generate points for the ellipse with found parameters, and add random noise to them:

```
pts = cv2.ellipse2Poly(center, axes, angle, 0, 360, 1)
pts += np.random.uniform(-10, 10, pts.shape).astype(np.int32)
```

4. Draw out the ellipse and generated points on the image, and display the image:

```
cv2.ellipse(img, center, axes, angle, 0, 360, (0, 255, 0), 3)

for pt in pts:
    cv2.circle(img, (int(pt[0]), int(pt[1])), 3, (0, 0, 255))

cv2.imshow('Fit ellipse', img)
cv2.waitKey()
cv2.destroyAllWindows()
```

5. Find the parameters of the ellipse which best fits our noisy points, draw the resulting ellipse on the image, and display it:

```
ellipse = cv2.fitEllipse(pts)
cv2.ellipse(img, ellipse, (0, 0, 0), 3)

cv2.imshow('Fit ellipse', img)
cv2.waitKey()
cv2.destroyAllWindows()
```

6. Create a clear image, generate points for the $y=x$ function, and add random noise to them:

```
img = np.full((512, 512, 3), 255, np.uint8)

pts = np.arange(512).reshape(-1, 1)
pts = np.hstack((pts, pts))
pts += np.random.uniform(-10, 10, pts.shape).astype(np.int32)
```

7. Draw the *y=x* function and generated points; then, display the image:

```
cv2.line(img, (0,0), (512, 512), (0, 255, 0), 3)

for pt in pts:
    cv2.circle(img, (int(pt[0]), int(pt[1])), 3, (0, 0, 255))

cv2.imshow('Fit line', img)
cv2.waitKey()
cv2.destroyAllWindows()
```

8. Find the parameters of the line for the noised points, draw the result, and display the image:

```
vx,vy,x,y = cv2.fitLine(pts, cv2.DIST_L2, 0, 0.01, 0.01)
y0 = int(y - x*vy/vx)
y1 = int((512 - x)*vy/vx + y)
cv2.line(img, (0, y0), (512, y1), (0, 0, 0), 3)

cv2.imshow('Fit line', img)
cv2.waitKey()
cv2.destroyAllWindows()
```

How it works...

In OpenCV, different functions are aimed at finding approximations for different types of curves: cv2.fitEllipse for ellipses and cv2.fitLine for lines. Both perform similar actions, minimize distances between points from the set we're fitting to the resulting curve, and require some minimal number of points to fit (five for cv2.fitEllipse and two for cv2.fitLine).

cv2.fitEllipse only accepts the argument of a set of two-dimensional points, for which we need to find curve parameters, and it returns the found ones, center point, half axes lengths, and rotation angle. These parameters can be directly passed to the cv2.ellipse drawing function when we want to display the result.

Another function, `cv2.line`, has more parameters. As previously, it takes a points set as its first argument, and also the type of distance function to minimize, the value to control distance functions, and the acceptable accuracy for the (*x0, y0*) point and the (*vx, vy*) line coefficients. (*x0, y0*) determines the point through which our line passes. The function returns (*x0, y0, vx, vy*) values for the line parameters which best fit the points set. It's important to mention that `cv2.line` is able to work not only with two-dimensional points, but with three-dimensional ones too, and the algorithm itself is robust to outliers in set-points, which are the result of huge noises or mistakes. Both facts make the routine very handy for practical usage. If we're passing three-dimensional points to `cv2.line`, we of course get the parameters of a three-dimensional line.

Calculating image moments

Image moments are statistical values computed from an image. They allow us to analyze the image as a whole. Note that it's often useful to extract contours first, and only then compute and work with each component moment, independently. In this recipe, you will learn how to compute moments for binary/grayscale images.

Getting ready

You need to have OpenCV 3.x installed, with Python API support.

How to do it...

1. Import the modules:

```
import cv2
import numpy as np
import matplotlib.pyplot as plt
```

2. Draw a test image—a white ellipse with the center at point (320, 240), on a black background:

```
image = np.zeros((480, 640), np.uint8)
cv2.ellipse(image, (320, 240), (200, 100), 0, 0, 360, 255, -1)
```

3. Compute the moments and print their values:

```
m = cv2.moments(image)
for name, val in m.items():
    print(name, '\t', val)
```

4. Perform a simple test to check whether the computed moments make sense, compute the center of the mass of the image using its first moments. It must be close to the center of the ellipse we specified above:

```
print('Center X estimated:', m['m10'] / m['m00'])
print('Center Y estimated:', m['m01'] / m['m00'])
```

How it works...

For binary or grayscale images, image moments are computed using the OpenCV function `cv2.moments`. It returns a dict of the calculated moments, with their respective names.

The following output is expected for the moments:

```
nu11      -2.809466679966455e-13
mu12      -422443285.20703125
mu21      -420182048.71875
m11       1237939564800.0
mu20      161575917357.31616
m10       5158101240.0
nu03      1.013174855849065e-10
nu12      -4.049505150683136e-10
nu21      -4.0278291313762605e-10
mu03      105694127.71875
nu30      1.618061841335058e-09
m30       683285449618080.0
nu02      0.00015660970937729079
m20       1812142855350.0
m00       16119315.0
mu02      40692263506.42969
nu20      0.0006218468887998859
m02       969157708320.0
m21       434912202354750.0
m01       3868620810.0
m03       252129278267070.0
mu11      -72.9990234375
mu30      1687957749.125
m12       310125260718570.0
```

The estimated center of mass is as follows:

```
Center X estimated: 319.9950643063927
Center Y estimated: 239.999082467214
```

 The definitions of different image moment types can be found at https://en.wikipedia.org/wiki/Image_moment.

Working with curves - approximation, length, and area

This recipe covers OpenCV functionality related to, features of curves. We will review the routines for computing a curve's length and area, getting the convex hull, and checking whether a curve is convex or not. Also, we will study how to approximate the contour with a smaller number of points. All of these things can be useful when you're developing an algorithm based on contour handling. By finding different features of the contour, you can build heuristics to filter out false contours. So, let's get started.

Getting ready

You need to have OpenCV 3.x installed, with Python API support.

How to do it...

1. Import all of the necessary modules, open an image, and display it on the screen:

```
import cv2, random
import numpy as np
img = cv2.imread('bw.png', cv2.IMREAD_GRAYSCALE)
```

2. Find the contours of the loaded image, draw them, and show the result:

```
im2, contours, hierarchy = cv2.findContours(img, cv2.RETR_TREE,
cv2.CHAIN_APPROX_SIMPLE)

color = cv2.cvtColor(img, cv2.COLOR_GRAY2BGR)
cv2.drawContours(color, contours, -1, (0,255,0), 3)
```

```
cv2.imshow('contours', color)
cv2.waitKey()
cv2.destroyAllWindows()
```

3. Take the first contour, find its area in various cases, and output the resulting numbers:

```
contour = contours[0]

print('Area of contour is %.2f' % cv2.contourArea(contour))
print('Signed area of contour is %.2f' % cv2.contourArea(contour,
True))
print('Signed area of contour is %.2f' %
cv2.contourArea(contour[::-1], True))
```

4. Find the length of the contour, and print it:

```
print('Length of closed contour is %.2f' % cv2.arcLength(contour,
True))
print('Length of open contour is %.2f' % cv2.arcLength(contour,
False))
```

5. Find the convex hull for the contour, draw it on the image, and display it:

```
hull = cv2.convexHull(contour)
cv2.drawContours(color, [hull], -1, (0,0,255), 3)

cv2.imshow('contours', color)
cv2.waitKey()
cv2.destroyAllWindows()
```

6. Check the convexity of the contour and its hull:

```
print('Convex status of contour is %s' %
cv2.isContourConvex(contour))
print('Convex status of its hull is %s' %
cv2.isContourConvex(hull))
```

7. Create a window with a trackbar to control the quality of contour approximation, find the approximation of the contour, and show the result:

```
cv2.namedWindow('contours')

img = np.copy(color)

def trackbar_callback(value):
    global img
```

```
        epsilon = value*cv2.arcLength(contour, True)*0.1/255
        approx = cv2.approxPolyDP(contour, epsilon, True)
        img = np.copy(color)
        cv2.drawContours(img, [approx], -1, (255,0,255), 3)

    cv2.createTrackbar('Epsilon', 'contours', 1, 255, lambda v:
    trackbar_callback(v))
    while True:
        cv2.imshow('contours', img)
        key = cv2.waitKey(3)
        if key == 27:
            break

    cv2.destroyAllWindows()
```

How it works...

cv2.contourArea computes the area of a contour, as implied by its name. It takes a point set which represents a contour as its first argument, and a Boolean flag as its second one. The routine returns the float-point area of the contour. The flag allows us to compute either the signed (when True) or unsigned (when False) area, where the sign stands for a clockwise or counter-clockwise order of points in the contour. An important note about cv2.contourArea is that it's not guaranteed that the area is correct for contours with self-intersection.

The function to get the length of a curve is cv2.arcLength. It accepts two parameters, a contour as a first argument, and a flag as a second. The flag controls the closedness of the contour, True means that the first and last points in the contour should be considered as connected, and therefore, the contour is closed. Otherwise, the distance between the first and last points doesn't account for the resulting contour perimeter.

cv2.convexHull helps you to find the convex hull of the contour. It takes the contour as an argument and returns its convex hull (which is also the contour). Also, you can check the convexity of a contour by using the cv2.isContourConvex function, just pass a contour as its argument, and the returned value will be True when the passed contour is convex.

To get a contour approximation, you should use the `cv2.approxPolyDP` function. This function implements the *Ramer–Douglas–Peucker* algorithm of finding a contour with fewer points, and some tolerance. It takes a contour (which should be approximated), tolerance (which is the maximum distance between the original contour and its approximation), and a Boolean flag (which tells the function whether to consider the approximated contour as closed). The larger the tolerance, the coarser the approximation, but the fewer points remain in the resulting contour. The function returns the approximation of the input contour for specified parameters.

You will see an image close to the one that follows as a result of the code execution:

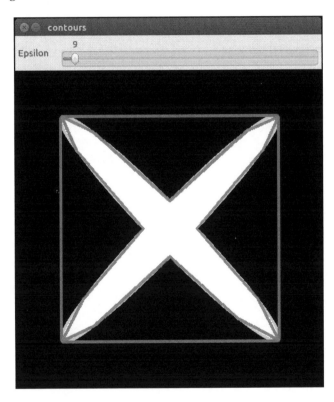

Checking whether a point is within a contour

In this recipe, we will discover a way of checking whether a point is inside of a contour, or if it belongs to the contour's border.

Getting ready

You need to have OpenCV 3.x installed, with Python API support.

How to do it...

1. Import all of the necessary modules, open an image, and display it on the screen:

```
import cv2, random
import numpy as np
img = cv2.imread('bw.png', cv2.IMREAD_GRAYSCALE)
```

2. Find the contours of the image and display them:

```
im2, contours, hierarchy = cv2.findContours(img, cv2.RETR_TREE,
cv2.CHAIN_APPROX_SIMPLE)

color = cv2.cvtColor(img, cv2.COLOR_GRAY2BGR)
cv2.drawContours(color, contours, -1, (0,255,0), 3)

cv2.imshow('contours', color)
cv2.waitKey()
cv2.destroyAllWindows()
```

3. Define a callback function to handle a user click on the image. This function draws a small circle where the click has happened, and the color of the circle is determined by whether the click was inside or outside of the contour:

```
contour = contours[0]
image_to_show = np.copy(color)
measure = True

def mouse_callback(event, x, y, flags, param):
    global contour, image_to_show
    if event == cv2.EVENT_LBUTTONUP:
        distance = cv2.pointPolygonTest(contour, (x,y), measure)
        image_to_show = np.copy(color)
```

```
        if distance > 0:
            pt_color = (0, 255, 0)
        elif distance < 0:
            pt_color = (0, 0, 255)
        else:
            pt_color = (128, 0, 128)
        cv2.circle(image_to_show, (x,y), 5, pt_color, -1)
        cv2.putText(image_to_show, '%.2f' % distance, (0,
image_to_show.shape[1] - 5),
                    cv2.FONT_HERSHEY_SIMPLEX, 1, (255, 255, 255))
```

4. Show the image with our mouse click handler. Also, let's track *M* button presses to switch the mode of what we get as a result of the `cv2.pointPolygonTest` function:

```
cv2.namedWindow('contours')
cv2.setMouseCallback('contours', mouse_callback)

while(True):
 cv2.imshow('contours', image_to_show)
 k = cv2.waitKey(1)

 if k == ord('m'):
     measure = not measure
 elif k == 27:
     break

cv2.destroyAllWindows()
```

How it works...

There is a special function in OpenCV to measure the smallest distance from a point to a contour. It's called `cv2.pointPolygonTest`. It takes three arguments, and returns the measured distance. The arguments are a contour, a point, and a Boolean flag, whose purpose we will discuss a little later. The resulting distance can be positive, negative, or equal to zero, which corresponds to inside the contour, outside the contour, or on a contour point position. The last Boolean argument determines whether our function returns the exact distance or only an indicator with a value (+1; 0; −1). The sign of the indicator has the same meaning as the mode that computes the exact distance.

As a result of the code, you will get something similar to this image:

Computing distance maps

In this recipe, you will learn how to compute the distance to the closest non-zero pixels from each image pixel. This functionality can be used to perform image processing in an adaptive way, for instance, for blurring an image with different strengths, depending on the distance to the closest edge.

Getting ready

Install the OpenCV 3.x Python API package and the `matplotlib` package.

How to do it...

1. Import the modules:

```
import cv2
import numpy as np
import matplotlib.pyplot as plt
```

2. Draw a test image—a black circle (without filling) on a white background:

```
image = np.full((480, 640), 255, np.uint8)
cv2.circle(image, (320, 240), 100, 0)
```

3. Compute the distance from every point to the circle:

```
distmap = cv2.distanceTransform(image, cv2.DIST_L2,
cv2.DIST_MASK_PRECISE)
```

4. Visualize the results:

```
plt.figure()
plt.imshow(distmap, cmap='gray')
plt.show()
```

How it works...

Distance maps can be calculated using the OpenCV `cv2.distanceTransform` function. It calculates the specified type of distance (`cv2.DIST_L1`, `cv2.DIST_L2`, or `cv2.DIST_C`) to the closest zero pixel. You can also vary the mask size that's used for computing the approximate distance (the available options are `cv2.DIST_MASK_3` and `cv2.DIST_MASK_5`). You can also use the `cv2.DIST_MASK_PRECISE` flag, which leads to computing not approximate, but precise distances.

The following output is expected:

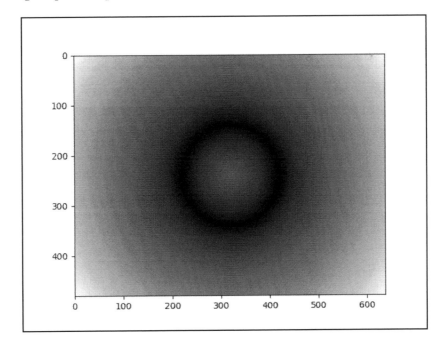

Image segmentation using the k-means algorithm

Sometimes, the color of pixels in an image can help determine where semantically close areas are. For example, road surfaces, in some circumstances, may have almost the same color. By color, we can find all road pixels. But what if we don't know the color of the road? Here, the k-means clustering algorithm comes into play. This algorithm only needs to know how many clusters are in an image, or, in other words, how many clusters we want an image to have. With this information, it can automatically find the best clusters. In this recipe, we will consider how k-means image segmentation can be applied using OpenCV.

Getting ready

Install the OpenCV 3.x Python API package and the `matplotlib` package.

How to do it...

1. Import the necessary modules:

```
import cv2
import numpy as np
import matplotlib.pyplot as plt
```

2. Open an image and convert it to Lab color space:

```
image = cv2.imread('../data/Lena.png').astype(np.float32) / 255.
image_lab = cv2.cvtColor(image, cv2.COLOR_BGR2Lab)
```

3. Reshape the image into a vector:

```
data = image_lab.reshape((-1, 3))
```

4. Define the number of clusters and the criteria to finish the segmentation process. Then, perform k-means clusterization:

```
num_classes = 4
criteria = (cv2.TERM_CRITERIA_EPS + cv2.TERM_CRITERIA_MAX_ITER, 50,
0.1)
_, labels, centers = cv2.kmeans(data, num_classes, None, criteria,
10, cv2.KMEANS_RANDOM_CENTERS)
```

5. Apply the colors of centroids to all pixels that are relevant to these centroids. Afterwards, reshape the segmented image back to its original shape. Then, convert it to RGB color space:

```
segmented_lab = centers[labels.flatten()].reshape(image.shape)
segmented = cv2.cvtColor(segmented_lab, cv2.COLOR_Lab2RGB)
```

6. Display the original and segmented images together:

```
plt.subplot(121)
plt.axis('off')
plt.title('original')
plt.imshow(image[:, :, [2, 1, 0]])
plt.subplot(122)
plt.axis('off')
plt.title('segmented')
plt.imshow(segmented)
plt.show()
```

How it works...

To perform k-means clusterization, we should use the `cv2.kmeans` function. It takes the following arguments, respectively, input data, the number of clusters, an input/output array with labels (can be set to `None`), stop process criteria, the number of attempts, and flags to control the process of clusterization.

Let's discuss each argument. The input data must be a vector of points with float values, in our case, we have three-dimensional points. The number of clusters determines how many of them we will get in the result, the greater the value, the greater the number of clusters, but the higher the influence of noise. The input/output array with labels can be used both to determine the initial positions of the clusters and to get the resulting clusters; if we don't want to specify cluster center initialization, we should set this argument to `None`. The stop process criteria determines how long the process of segmentation works when trying to find the best cluster positions. The number of attempts defines how many times the clusterization process will be launched from different cluster initializations, to later choose the best attempt. And the flags determine the type of cluster initialization; it can be `cv2.KMEANS_RANDOM_CENTERS` for random initialization, `cv2.KMEANS_PP_CENTERS` for more sophisticated initialization, (kmeans++ algorithm) and `cv2.KMEANS_USE_INITIAL_LABELS` to pass user specified cluster centers (in this case, the third argument can't be None).

The function returns a double value for the compactness for each cluster, a vector with labels, and values for each label. The compactness of a cluster is the sum of the squared distance from each cluster point to the corresponding center. The vector with labels has the same length as the input data vector, and each of its elements represents an output cluster which has been set to the corresponding position in the input data. The values for each label are values for centers of clusters.

In this recipe, Lab color space was used, due to its property of separating color information and brightness information. In RGB space, color and brightness are mixed together across all channels, but this can negatively influence the segmentation process.

Note that when working with `uint8` images, OpenCV applies linear processing to Lab color space values. So, one must be careful when converting between color spaces. In the case of `float32` images, pixel values must be left unchanged. See `https://docs.opencv.org/master/de/d25/imgproc_color_conversions.html`.

After launching the code, you will get images similar to the following:

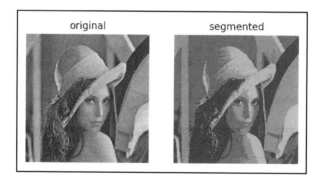

Image segmentation using segment seeds - the watershed algorithm

The watershed algorithm of image segmentation is used when we have initial segmented points and want to automatically fill surrounding areas with the same segmentation class. These initial segmented points are called seeds, and they should be set manually, but in some cases, it's possible to automatically assign them. This recipe shows how to implement the watershed segmentation algorithm in OpenCV.

Getting ready

Install the OpenCV 3.x Python API package and the `matplotlib` package.

How to do it...

1. Import the necessary modules and functions:

```
import cv2, random
import numpy as np
from random import randint
```

2. Load an image to segment and create its copy and other images to store seeds and the segmentation result:

```
img = cv2.imread('../data/Lena.png')
show_img = np.copy(img)

seeds = np.full(img.shape[0:2], 0, np.int32)
segmentation = np.full(img.shape, 0, np.uint8)
```

3. Define the number of seed types, the color for each seed type, and some variables to work with mouse events:

```
n_seeds = 9

colors = []
for m in range(n_seeds):
    colors.append((255 * m / n_seeds, randint(0, 255), randint(0, 255)))

mouse_pressed = False
current_seed = 1
seeds_updated = False
```

4. Implement the mouse callback function to handle events from the mouse; let's draw seeds on the image by dragging the mouse with a pressed button:

```
def mouse_callback(event, x, y, flags, param):
    global mouse_pressed, seeds_updated

    if event == cv2.EVENT_LBUTTONDOWN:
        mouse_pressed = True
        cv2.circle(seeds, (x, y), 5, (current_seed), cv2.FILLED)
```

```
            cv2.circle(show_img, (x, y), 5, colors[current_seed - 1],
            cv2.FILLED)
            seeds_updated = True

        elif event == cv2.EVENT_MOUSEMOVE:
            if mouse_pressed:
                cv2.circle(seeds, (x, y), 5, (current_seed),
    cv2.FILLED)
                cv2.circle(show_img, (x, y), 5, colors[current_seed -
                1], cv2.FILLED)
                seeds_updated = True

        elif event == cv2.EVENT_LBUTTONUP:
            mouse_pressed = False
```

5. Create all of the necessary windows, set the callbacks, display the images, and track the keyboard buttons pressed in the loop. Let's change the current seed to draw by pressing numbers. And, when the seed changing process is finished, segment the image with the watershed algorithm:

```
cv2.namedWindow('image')
cv2.setMouseCallback('image', mouse_callback)

while True:
    cv2.imshow('segmentation', segmentation)
    cv2.imshow('image', show_img)
    k = cv2.waitKey(1)

    if k == 27:
        break
    elif k == ord('c'):
        show_img = np.copy(img)
        seeds = np.full(img.shape[0:2], 0, np.int32)
        segmentation = np.full(img.shape, 0, np.uint8)
    elif k > 0 and chr(k).isdigit():
        n = int(chr(k))
        if 1 <= n <= n_seeds and not mouse_pressed:
            current_seed = n
    if seeds_updated and not mouse_pressed:
        seeds_copy = np.copy(seeds)
        cv2.watershed(img, seeds_copy)
        segmentation = np.full(img.shape, 0, np.uint8)
        for m in range(n_seeds):
            segmentation[seeds_copy == (m + 1)] = colors[m]
        seeds_updated = False
cv2.destroyAllWindows()
```

How it works...

The `cv2.watershed` function implements the algorithm and takes two arguments, the image to segment and the initial seeds. The segmented image should be color and 8-bit. Seeds should be stored in the image, with the same spatial size as the segmented image, but with only one channel and a different depth, `int32`. Different seeds should be represented in the second argument, with different numbers, and other pixels should be set to zero. The routine fills zero values in the seed image with relevant neighbor seeds.

After launching the code from this recipe, you will see an image similar to the following:

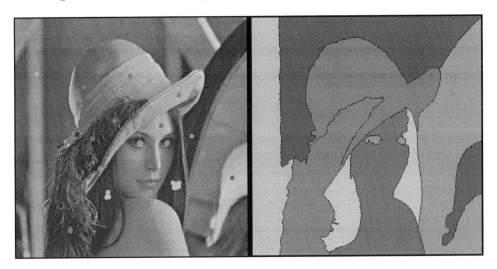

4
Object Detection and Machine Learning

In this chapter, we will cover the following recipes:

- Obtaining an object mask using the GrabCut algorithm
- Finding edges using the Canny algorithm
- Detecting lines and circles using the Hough transform
- Finding objects via template matching
- The real-time median-flow object tracker
- Tracking objects using different algorithms via the tracking API
- Computing the dense optical flow between two frames
- Detecting chessboard and circle grid patterns
- A simple pedestrian detector using the SVM model
- Optical character recognition using different machine learning models
- Detecting faces using Haar/LBP cascades
- Detecting AruCo patterns for AR applications
- Detecting text in natural scenes
- The QR code detector and recognizer

Introduction

Our world contains a lot of objects. Each type of object has its own features that distinguish it from some types and, at the same time, make it similar to others. Understanding the scene through the objects in it is a key task in computer vision. Being able to find and track various objects, detect basic patterns and complex structures, and recognize text are challenging and useful skills, and this chapter addresses questions on how to implement and use them with OpenCV functionality.

We will review the detection of geometric primitives, such as lines, circles, and chessboards, and more complex objects, such as pedestrians, faces, AruCo, and QR code patterns. We will also perform object tracking tasks.

Obtaining an object mask using the GrabCut algorithm

There are cases where we want to separate an object from other parts of a scene; in other words, where we want to create masks for the foreground and background. This job is tackled by the GrabCut algorithm. It can build object masks in semi-automatic mode. All that it needs are initial assumptions about object location. Based on these assumptions, the algorithm performs a multi-step iterative procedure to model statistical distributions of foreground and background pixels and find the best division according to the distributions. This sounds complicated, but the usage is very simple. Let's find out how easily we can apply this sophisticated algorithm in OpenCV.

Getting ready

Before you proceed with this recipe, you need to install the OpenCV 3.x Python API package.

How to do it...

1. Import the modules:

```
import cv2
import numpy as np
```

2. Open an image and define the mouse callback function to draw a rectangle on the image:

```python
img = cv2.imread('../data/Lena.png', cv2.IMREAD_COLOR)
show_img = np.copy(img)

mouse_pressed = False
y = x = w = h = 0

def mouse_callback(event, _x, _y, flags, param):
    global show_img, x, y, w, h, mouse_pressed

    if event == cv2.EVENT_LBUTTONDOWN:
        mouse_pressed = True
        x, y = _x, _y
        show_img = np.copy(img)

    elif event == cv2.EVENT_MOUSEMOVE:
        if mouse_pressed:
            show_img = np.copy(img)
            cv2.rectangle(show_img, (x, y),
                          (_x, _y), (0, 255, 0), 3)

    elif event == cv2.EVENT_LBUTTONUP:
        mouse_pressed = False
        w, h = _x - x, _y - y
```

3. Display the image, and, after the rectangle has been completed and the *A* button on the keyboard has been pressed, close the window with the following code:

```python
cv2.namedWindow('image')
cv2.setMouseCallback('image', mouse_callback)

while True:
    cv2.imshow('image', show_img)
    k = cv2.waitKey(1)

    if k == ord('a') and not mouse_pressed:
        if w*h > 0:
            break

cv2.destroyAllWindows()
```

4. Call `cv2.grabCut` to create an object mask based on the rectangle that was drawn. Then, create the object mask and define it as:

```
labels = np.zeros(img.shape[:2],np.uint8)

labels, bgdModel, fgdModel = cv2.grabCut(img, labels, (x, y, w, h),
None, None, 5, cv2.GC_INIT_WITH_RECT)

show_img = np.copy(img)
show_img[(labels == cv2.GC_PR_BGD)|(labels == cv2.GC_BGD)] //= 3

cv2.imshow('image', show_img)
cv2.waitKey()
cv2.destroyAllWindows()
```

5. Define the mouse callback to draw the mask on the image. It's necessary to repair mistakes in the previous `cv2.grabCut` call:

```
label = cv2.GC_BGD
lbl_clrs = {cv2.GC_BGD: (0,0,0), cv2.GC_FGD: (255,255,255)}

def mouse_callback(event, x, y, flags, param):
    global mouse_pressed

    if event == cv2.EVENT_LBUTTONDOWN:
        mouse_pressed = True
        cv2.circle(labels, (x, y), 5, label, cv2.FILLED)
        cv2.circle(show_img, (x, y), 5, lbl_clrs[label],
cv2.FILLED)

    elif event == cv2.EVENT_MOUSEMOVE:
        if mouse_pressed:
            cv2.circle(labels, (x, y), 5, label, cv2.FILLED)
            cv2.circle(show_img, (x, y), 5, lbl_clrs[label],
cv2.FILLED)

    elif event == cv2.EVENT_LBUTTONUP:
        mouse_pressed = False
```

6. Show the image with the mask; use white to draw where the object pixels have been labeled as a background, and use black to draw where the background areas have been marked as belonging to the object. Then, call `cv2.grabCut` again to get the fixed mask. Finally, update the mask on the image, and show it:

```
cv2.namedWindow('image')
cv2.setMouseCallback('image', mouse_callback)
```

```
while True:
    cv2.imshow('image', show_img)
    k = cv2.waitKey(1)

    if k == ord('a') and not mouse_pressed:
        break
    elif k == ord('l'):
        label = cv2.GC_FGD - label

cv2.destroyAllWindows()

labels, bgdModel, fgdModel = cv2.grabCut(img, labels, None,
bgdModel, fgdModel, 5, cv2.GC_INIT_WITH_MASK)

show_img = np.copy(img)
show_img[(labels == cv2.GC_PR_BGD)|(labels == cv2.GC_BGD)] //= 3

cv2.imshow('image', show_img)
cv2.waitKey()
cv2.destroyAllWindows()
```

How it works...

OpenCV's `cv2.grabCut` implements the GrabCut algorithm. This function is able to work in several modes, and takes the following arguments: input 3-channel image, a matrix with initial labels for pixels, a rectangle in (*x*, *y*, *w*, *h*) format to define label initialization, two matrices to store the process state, a number of iterations, and the mode in which we want the function to launch.

The function returns labels matrix and two matrices with the state of the process. The labels matrix is single-channel, and it stores one of these values in each pixel: `cv2.GC_BGD` (this means that the pixel definitely belongs to the background), `cv2.GC_PR_BGD` (this means that the pixel is probably in the background), `cv2.GC_PR_FGD` (for pixels which are possibly foreground), `cv2.GC_FGD` (for pixels which are definitely foreground). The two state matrices are necessary if we want to continue the process for a few iterations.

There are three possible modes for the function: `cv2.GC_INIT_WITH_RECT`, `cv2.GC_INIT_WITH_MASK` and `cv2.GC_EVAL`. The first one is used when we want to define labels initialization by the rectangle in the third argument. In this case, pixels outside of the rectangle are set to the `cv2.GC_BGD` value, and ones inside the rectangle are set to the `cv2.GC_PR_FGD` value.

The second mode of the function, `cv2.GC_INIT_WITH_MASK`, is used when we want to use the values of the second argument matrix as initialization for labels. In this case, the values should be set to one of four values: `cv2.GC_BGD`, `cv2.GC_PR_BGD`, `cv2.GC_PR_FGD`, or `cv2.GC_FGD`.

The third mode, `cv2.GC_EVAL`, is for calling the function for another number of iterations, with the same state.

In the code, we darken the background to visualize the object mask. It works well when the object we want to segment has similar brightness to other parts of the image. But, in the case of a dark object on a bright scene, it won't work. So, you may need to apply another visualization technique in your own project.

As a result of launching the code, you will get pictures similar to the following:

Finding edges using the Canny algorithm

Edges are a useful image feature that can be used in many computer vision applications. In this recipe, you will learn how to detect edges in images using the Canny algorithm.

Getting ready

Install the OpenCV 3.x Python API package and the `matplotlib` package.

How to do it...

Here are the steps needed to complete this recipe:

1. Import the modules:

```
import cv2
import matplotlib.pyplot as plt
```

2. Load the test image:

```
image = cv2.imread('../data/Lena.png')
```

3. Detect the edges using the Canny algorithm:

```
edges = cv2.Canny(image, 200, 100)
```

4. Visualize the results:

```
plt.figure(figsize=(8,5))
plt.subplot(121)
plt.axis('off')
plt.title('original')
plt.imshow(image[:,:,[2,1,0]])
plt.subplot(122)
plt.axis('off')
plt.title('edges')
plt.imshow(edges, cmap='gray')
plt.tight_layout()
plt.show()
```

How it works...

Canny edge detection is a very powerful and popular tool in computer vision. It's named after John F. Canny, who proposed the algorithm in 1986. OpenCV implements the algorithm in the function `cv2.Canny`. You must specify two thresholds for gradient magnitude in this function: the first one is used for detecting strong edges, and the second one is used for the hysteresis procedure, where the strong edges are being grown.

The following output is expected:

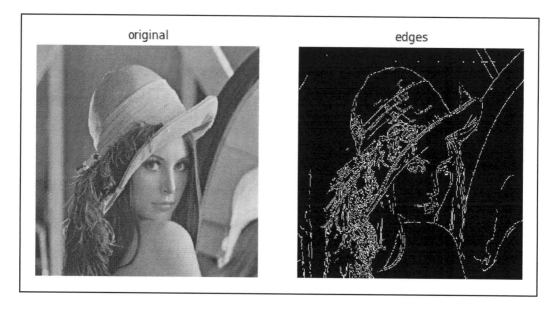

Detecting lines and circles using the Hough transform

In this recipe, you will learn how to apply the Hough transform for the detection of lines and circles. This is a helpful technique when you need to perform basic image analysis and find primitives in images.

Getting ready

Before you proceed with this recipe, you need to install the OpenCV 3.x Python API package and the `matplotlib` package.

How to do it...

1. Import the modules:

```
import cv2
import numpy as np
```

2. Draw a test image:

```
img = np.zeros((500, 500), np.uint8)
cv2.circle(img, (200, 200), 50, 255, 3)
cv2.line(img, (100, 400), (400, 350), 255, 3)
```

3. Detect lines using the probabilistic Hough transform:

```
lines = cv2.HoughLinesP(img, 1, np.pi/180, 100, 100, 10)[0]
```

4. Detect circles using the Hough transform:

```
circles = cv2.HoughCircles(img, cv2.HOUGH_GRADIENT, 1, 15,
param1=200, param2=30)[0]
```

5. Draw the detected lines and circles:

```
dbg_img = np.zeros((img.shape[0], img.shape[1], 3), np.uint8)
for x1, y1, x2, y2 in lines:
    print('Detected line: ({} {}) ({} {})'.format(x1, y1, x2, y2))
    cv2.line(dbg_img, (x1, y1), (x2, y2), (0, 255, 0), 2)

for c in circles:
    print('Detected circle: center=({} {}), radius={}'.format(c[0],
c[1], c[2]))
    cv2.circle(dbg_img, (c[0], c[1]), c[2], (0, 255, 0), 2)
```

6. Visualize the results:

```
plt.figure(figsize=(8,4))
plt.subplot(121)
plt.title('original')
plt.axis('off')
plt.imshow(img, cmap='gray')
plt.subplot(122)
plt.title('detected primitives')
plt.axis('off')
plt.imshow(dbg_img)
plt.show()
```

How it works...

The Hough transform is a technique for the detection of any shapes parametrized and represented in a convenient mathematical form. Basically, for every pixel in a source image, the Hough transform finds a set of model parameters that satisfy the observation and stores them in table. Each pixel votes for a subset of possible models. Output detections are obtained via a voting procedure.

The detection of lines is implemented in the function `cv2.HoughLineP`. In fact, it does not implement the original Hough transform, but its optimized, probabilistic version. The function takes parameters such as the source image, voting space spatial resolution, voting space angular resolution, minimum votes threshold, minimum line length, and maximum allowed gap between points on the same line to link them, and returns a list of detected lines represented in a `start_point`, `end_point` form.

The detection of circles is implemented in the function `cv2.HoughCircles`. It takes the input source image, detection method (only `cv2.HOUGH_GRADIENT` is supported, for now), inverse voting space resolution, minimum distance between the centers of detected circles, and two optional parameters: the first is the higher threshold for the Canny edge detection procedure, and the second is the votes count threshold.

The following output is expected for the preceding code:

```
Detected line: (99 401) (372 353)
Detected circle: center=(201.5 198.5), radius=50.400001525878906
```

The output looks as follows:

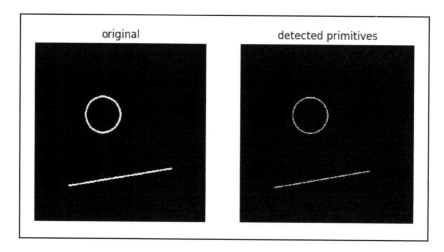

Finding objects via template matching

Finding an object in the image isn't a simple task, due to various representations the same instance may look dramatically different, and at first sight, some complicated computer vision algorithms are required. But, if we limit the issue, the task may be successfully solved by relatively simple methods. In this recipe, we consider the methods for finding objects on the image which correspond to some of the template.

Getting ready

Before you proceed with this recipe, you need to install the OpenCV 3.x Python API package.

How to do it...

Perform the following steps:

1. Import the modules:

```
import cv2
import numpy as np
```

2. Load image and define mouse callback function for selecting image ROI. What is inside of the rectangle that is drawn will be our template for matching:

```
img = cv2.imread('../data/Lena.png', cv2.IMREAD_COLOR)
show_img = np.copy(img)

mouse_pressed = False
y = x = w = h = 0

def mouse_callback(event, _x, _y, flags, param):
    global show_img, x, y, w, h, mouse_pressed

    if event == cv2.EVENT_LBUTTONDOWN:
        mouse_pressed = True
        x, y = _x, _y
        show_img = np.copy(img)

    elif event == cv2.EVENT_MOUSEMOVE:
        if mouse_pressed:
            show_img = np.copy(img)
```

```
cv2.rectangle(show_img, (x, y),
              (_x, _y), (0, 255, 0), 2)

elif event == cv2.EVENT_LBUTTONUP:
    mouse_pressed = False
    w, h = _x - x, _y - y
```

3. Display the image, select an object to find with the mouse, and press the *A* button to finish the process and get the template:

```
cv2.namedWindow('image')
cv2.setMouseCallback('image', mouse_callback)

while True:
    cv2.imshow('image', show_img)
    k = cv2.waitKey(1)

    if k == ord('a') and not mouse_pressed:
        if w*h > 0:
            break

cv2.destroyAllWindows()

template = np.copy(img[y:y+h, x:x+w])
```

4. Show the image and handle button press events. Digits from 0 to 5 determine the method we use to find areas on the image which are similar to the template. The matching is performed with the `cv2.matchTemplate` function. When the matching is finished, we find the points with the highest (or the lowest) similarity metric and draw detection results:

```
methods = ['cv2.TM_CCOEFF', 'cv2.TM_CCOEFF_NORMED', 'cv2.TM_CCORR',
           'cv2.TM_CCORR_NORMED', 'cv2.TM_SQDIFF',
'cv2.TM_SQDIFF_NORMED']

show_img = np.copy(img)

while True:
    cv2.imshow('image', show_img)
    k = cv2.waitKey()

    if k == 27:
        break
    elif k > 0 and chr(k).isdigit():
        index = int(chr(k))
        if 0 <= index < len(methods):
            method = methods[index]
```

```
res = cv2.matchTemplate(img, template, eval(method))
res = cv2.normalize(res, None, 0, 1, cv2.NORM_MINMAX)
if index >= methods.index('cv2.TM_SQDIFF'):
    loc = np.where(res < 0.01)
else:
    loc = np.where(res > 0.99)
show_img = np.copy(img)
for pt in zip(*loc[::-1]):
    cv2.rectangle(show_img, pt, (pt[0] + w, pt[1] + h),
                  (0, 0, 255), 2)
res = cv2.resize(res, show_img.shape[:2])*255
res = cv2.cvtColor(res,
cv2.COLOR_GRAY2BGR).astype(np.uint8)
        cv2.putText(res, method, (0, 30),
cv2.FONT_HERSHEY_SIMPLEX,
                    1, (0, 0, 255), 3)
    show_img = np.hstack((show_img, res))

cv2.destroyAllWindows()
```

How it works...

`cv2.matchTemplate` is used to find image regions that are similar to the template. The similarity can be determined with different methods (different mathematical operations to get the difference between the template and a patch on the image). But, none of these methods are able to find templates with different scales or orientations.

This function takes source image, search template, and the method of patch and template comparison. The methods are determined by these values: `cv2.TM_CCOEFF`, `cv2.TM_CCOEFF_NORMED`, `cv2.TM_CCORR`, `cv2.TM_CCORR_NORMED`, `cv2.TM_SQDIFF` or `cv2.TM_SQDIFF_NORMED`. The methods with `CCOEFF` in the name use correlation coefficient computation, like the similarity measure—the bigger the value, the more similar the regions are. The methods with `CCORR` use cross-correlation computation to compare patches, and the methods with `SQDIFF` find the square difference between the regions to compare them.

The function returns the distribution of the selected similarity metric across the input image. The returned image is a single-channel floating point, with a spatial size (W-w+1, H-h+1), where capital letters stand for input image dimensions and small letters are for template dimensions. The content of the returned image depends on the method we use, for approaches with correlation computation, a bigger value means better matching. And, as the name implies, the methods with square difference usage have the smallest values as perfect matches.

Methods which use correlation coefficient computation give the fewest mismatches, but require more computation. Square difference methods take less computation, but also give less reliable results. This can be application for small and/or featureless patches, as shown on the second image that follows.

After code execution, you will get something similar to the following images (depending on the template and the method you've selected):

The medial flow tracker

In this recipe, we're going to apply the Median Flow object tracker to track objects in a video. This tracker works in real time (even faster on modern hardware) and does its job accurately and steadily. Also, this tracker has a nice feature, it can determine the tracking failure. Let's see how we can use it in our applications.

Getting ready

Before you proceed with this recipe, you need to install the OpenCV 3.x Python API package with the OpenCV Contrib modules.

How to do it...

The steps for this recipe are:

1. Import all of the necessary modules:

```
import cv2
import numpy as np
```

2. Open a video file, read its frame, and select an object to track:

```
cap = cv2.VideoCapture("../data/traffic.mp4")

_, frame = cap.read()

bbox = cv2.selectROI(frame, False, True)

cv2.destroyAllWindows()
```

3. Create the Median Flow tracker and initialize it with the first frame from the video and the bounding box we've selected. Then, read the remaining frames one-by-one, feed them into the tracker, and get a new bounding box for each frame. Display the bounding box, as well as the number of frames that the Median Flow algorithm is able to process each second:

```
tracker = cv2.TrackerMedianFlow_create()
status_tracker = tracker.init(frame, bbox)
fps = 0

while True:
```

```
        status_cap, frame = cap.read()
        if not status_cap:
            break

        if status_tracker:
            timer = cv2.getTickCount()
            status_tracker, bbox = tracker.update(frame)
        if status_tracker:
            x, y, w, h = [int(i) for i in bbox]
            cv2.rectangle(frame, (x, y), (x + w, y + h), (0, 255, 0),
15)
            fps = cv2.getTickFrequency() / (cv2.getTickCount() -
timer);
            cv2.putText(frame, "FPS: %.0f" % fps, (0, 80),
cv2.FONT_HERSHEY_SIMPLEX, 3.5, (0, 0, 0), 8);
        else:
            cv2.putText(frame, "Tracking failure detected", (0, 80),
cv2.FONT_HERSHEY_SIMPLEX, 3.5, (0,0,255), 8)
        cv2.imshow("MedianFlow tracker", frame)

        k = cv2.waitKey(1)
        if k == 27:
            break
cv2.destroyAllWindows()
```

How it works...

To create the Median Flow tracker, we need to use `cv2.TrackerMedianFlow_create`. This function returns an instance of our tracker. Next, the tracker should be initialized with the object to follow. This can be done with the `init` function call. This function should be invoked for the tracker instance with the following arguments: the frame with the object to track and the bounding box of the object in an (x, y, width, height) format. The function returns `True` if initialization has been completed successfully.

When we have a new frame, we want to get a new bounding box for the object. To do this, we need to call the tracker instance's `update` function, with the new frame as an argument. The values returned from this routine are the tracker status and the new bounding box, still in an (x, y, width, height) format. The status of the tracker is a Boolean variable, which shows if the tracker continues to track the object or if the tracking process has failed.

It is worthwhile to mention the `cv2.selectROI` function. It helps you to easily choose regions on the image with the mouse and keyboard. It accepts image where we want to select ROI, flag indicating if we want to grid, flag specifying ROI selection mode, either from the top-left corner or from the center. After calling this function, the image will appear on the screen, and you will be able to click and drag your mouse to draw a rectangle. When the process of selection is completed, just hit the whitespace key on the keyboard, and you will get the parameters of the selected rectangle as a returned value.

After launching the preceding code and selecting an object, you will see how the object is being tracked in the video. The following shows a few frames, with tracking results:

As you can see, this tracker successfully handles changes in object scale and reports when a tracked object is lost.

Tracking objects using different algorithms via the tracking API

In this recipe, you will learn how to use the different tracking algorithms implemented in the OpenCV tracking contrib module. Different tracking algorithms have different properties in terms of accuracy, reliability, and speed. Using the tracking API, you can try to find the one that best suits your needs.

Getting ready

Before you proceed with this recipe, you need to install the OpenCV 3.x Python API package and the matplotlib package. OpenCV must be built with contrib modules, because the tracking API isn't a part of the main OpenCV repo.

How to do it...

To complete this recipe, perform the following steps:

1. Import the module:

```
import cv2
```

2. Create the main window and loop over the different trackers:

```
cv2.namedWindow('frame')

for name, tracker in (('KCF', cv2.TrackerKCF_create),
                      ('MIL', cv2.TrackerMIL_create),
                      ('TLD', cv2.TrackerTLD_create)):
    tracker = tracker()
    initialized = False
```

3. Open the test video file and select an object:

```
video = cv2.VideoCapture('../data/traffic.mp4')
bbox = (878, 266, 1153-878, 475-266)
```

4. Track until the video ends or *ESC* is pressed, and visualize the current tracked object:

```
while True:
    t0 = time.time()
    ok, frame = video.read()
    if not ok:
        break

    if initialized:
        tracked, bbox = tracker.update(frame)
    else:
        cv2.imwrite('/tmp/frame.png', frame)
        tracked = tracker.init(frame, bbox)
        initialized = True

    fps = 1 / (time.time() - t0)
    cv2.putText(frame, 'tracker: {}, fps: {:.1f}'.format(name, fps),
                (10, 50), cv2.FONT_HERSHEY_SIMPLEX, 1, (255, 0, 0), 2)
    if tracked:
        bbox = tuple(map(int, bbox))
        cv2.rectangle(frame, (bbox[0], bbox[1]),
```

```
                              (bbox[0]+bbox[2], bbox[1]+bbox[3]),
                              (0, 255, 0), 3)
            cv2.imshow('frame', frame)
            if cv2.waitKey(3) == 27:
                break
```

5. Close the windows:

```
    cv2.destroyAllWindows()
```

How it works...

The OpenCV tracking API provides access to many different tracking algorithms, such as Median Flow, **Kernelized correlation filters (KCF)**, **Tracking-Learning-Detection (TLD)**, and some others. A tracker can be instantiated via the `cv2.TrackerKCF_create` method (instead of KCF, you can specify any other supported tracking algorithm name). The tracking model must be initialized for the first frame, with the initial object position specified via the method `tracker.init`. After that, each frame must be processed with the method `tracker.update`, which returns the tracking status and current position of the tracked object.

The following output is expected after a few steps (the frame rate figures are, obviously, hardware dependent):

Computing the dense optical flow between two frames

The optical flow is a family of algorithms which addresses the issue of finding the movement of points between two images (usually subsequent frames in a video). Dense optical flow algorithms find movements of all pixels in a frame. The dense optical flow can be used to find objects moving in a sequence of frames, or to detect camera movements. In this recipe, we will find out how to compute and display the dense optical flow in several ways, using OpenCV functionality.

Getting ready

Before you proceed with this recipe, you need to install the OpenCV 3.x Python API package.

How to do it...

You need to perform the following steps:

1. Import the modules we're going to use:

```
import cv2
import numpy as np
```

2. Define the function to display the optical flow:

```
def display_flow(img, flow, stride=40):
    for index in np.ndindex(flow[::stride, ::stride].shape[:2]):
        pt1 = tuple(i*stride for i in index)
        delta = flow[pt1].astype(np.int32)[::-1]
        pt2 = tuple(pt1 + 10*delta)
        if 2 <= cv2.norm(delta) <= 10:
            cv2.arrowedLine(img, pt1[::-1], pt2[::-1], (0,0,255),
5, cv2.LINE_AA, 0, 0.4)
    norm_opt_flow = np.linalg.norm(flow, axis=2)
    norm_opt_flow = cv2.normalize(norm_opt_flow, None, 0, 1,
cv2.NORM_MINMAX)
    cv2.imshow('optical flow', img)
    cv2.imshow('optical flow magnitude', norm_opt_flow)
    k = cv2.waitKey(1)
    if k == 27:
```

```
        return 1
    else:
        return 0
```

3. Open the video and grab its first frame. Next, read the frames one-by-one and compute the dense optical flow using Gunnar Farneback's algorithm. Then, display the results:

```
cap = cv2.VideoCapture("../data/traffic.mp4")
_, prev_frame = cap.read()

prev_frame = cv2.cvtColor(prev_frame, cv2.COLOR_BGR2GRAY)
prev_frame = cv2.resize(prev_frame, (0,0), None, 0.5, 0.5)
init_flow = True

while True:
    status_cap, frame = cap.read()
    frame = cv2.resize(frame, (0,0), None, 0.5, 0.5)
    if not status_cap:
        break
    gray = cv2.cvtColor(frame, cv2.COLOR_BGR2GRAY)
    if init_flow:
        opt_flow = cv2.calcOpticalFlowFarneback(prev_frame, gray,
None,
                                                0.5, 5, 13, 10, 5,
1.1,
cv2.OPTFLOW_FARNEBACK_GAUSSIAN)
        init_flow = False
    else:
        opt_flow = cv2.calcOpticalFlowFarneback(prev_frame, gray,
opt_flow,
                                                0.5, 5, 13, 10, 5,
1.1,
cv2.OPTFLOW_USE_INITIAL_FLOW)
    prev_frame = np.copy(gray)
    if display_flow(frame, opt_flow):
        break;
cv2.destroyAllWindows()
```

4. Set the position of the video capture to the beginning, and read the first frame. Create an instance of a class which computes the Dual TV L1 optical flow. Then, read the frames one-by-one and get the optical flow for each subsequent pair of frames; display the results:

```
cap.set(cv2.CAP_PROP_POS_FRAMES, 0)
_, prev_frame = cap.read()
```

```
prev_frame = cv2.cvtColor(prev_frame, cv2.COLOR_BGR2GRAY)
prev_frame = cv2.resize(prev_frame, (0,0), None, 0.5, 0.5)

flow_DualTVL1 = cv2.createOptFlow_DualTVL1()

while True:
    status_cap, frame = cap.read()
    frame = cv2.resize(frame, (0,0), None, 0.5, 0.5)
    if not status_cap:
        break
    gray = cv2.cvtColor(frame, cv2.COLOR_BGR2GRAY)
    if not flow_DualTVL1.getUseInitialFlow():
        opt_flow = flow_DualTVL1.calc(prev_frame, gray, None)
        flow_DualTVL1.setUseInitialFlow(True)
    else:
        opt_flow = flow_DualTVL1.calc(prev_frame, gray, opt_flow)
    prev_frame = np.copy(gray)
    if display_flow(frame, opt_flow):
        break;
cv2.destroyAllWindows()
```

How it works...

To compute the optical flow, you need two images (which are usually consecutive frames from a video). Both methods that we've used in the code accept 8-bit grayscale images as frames.

First, let's discuss the usage of the `cv2.calcOpticalFlowFarneback` function. It takes the following parameters, the previous frame, current frame, initialization for optical flow, scale between the pyramid's layers, number of layers in the pyramid, size of the window for the smoothing step, number of iterations, number of neighborhood pixels to find the polynom's parameters, standard deviation of Gaussian (which is used to smooth the polynom's derivatives), and finally, flags.

The last parameter manages the optical flow process,
if `cv2.OPTFLOW_FARNEBACK_GAUSSIAN` is used, then input images are blurred with a Gaussian filter and the size of the window equals the value of the sixth argument;
if `cv2.OPTFLOW_USE_INITIAL_FLOW` is used, then the algorithm considers the third argument as an initialization of optical flow—which is used, then, we handle frames till a video and have the optical flow computed beforehand. Flags can be combined using a logical OR operation.

Referring to the remaining arguments, the values used in the code are considered good for the algorithm, so it's possible to use them as-is; in most of the cases, they work well.

Applying the Dual TV L1 optical flow algorithm is different. We need to create an instance of the `cv2.DualTVL1OpticalFlow` class by calling the `cv2.createOptFlow_DualTVL1` function. Then, we can get the optical flow by calling the `calc` function of the created instance. This function takes the previous frame, current frame, and optical flow initialization as arguments.

To get or set the values of algorithm parameters, you need to use class functions. As seen previously, most of the parameters are initialized with values that work well in many cases. The one that you need to change is the parameter of optical flow initialization. It can be done with the `setUseInitialFlow` function.

Both functions return the optical flow as a result of computation. It is presented as a 2-channel matrix of floating-point values, and has the same spatial size as the input frames. The first channel consists of the X (horizontal) projection of the movement vector for each frame pixel; the second channel is for the Y (vertical) projection of the movement vector. So, we are able to know the direction of the movement for each pixel, as well as the magnitude.

You will get the following images as a result of the preceding code. The first image is for Farneback's algorithm:

The second image is for Dual TV L1:

As you can see, Dual TV L1 gives the optical flow without holes, compared to Farneback's algorithm. But it costs computing time, the Dual TV L1 algorimth is much slower.

Detecting chessboard and circle grid patterns

In this recipe, you will learn how to detect chessboard and circle grid patterns. These patterns are very useful in computer vision, and are often used for estimating camera parameters.

Getting ready

Before you proceed with this recipe, you need to install the OpenCV 3.x Python API package and the `matplotlib` package.

How to do it...

1. Import the modules:

```
import cv2
import matplotlib.pyplot as plt
```

2. Load the test image with a chessboard:

```
image_chess = cv2.imread('../data/chessboard.png')
```

3. Detect the chessboard pattern:

```
found, corners = cv2.findChessboardCorners(image_chess, (6, 9))
assert found == True, "can't find chessboard pattern"
```

4. Draw the detected pattern:

```
dbg_image_chess = image_chess.copy()
cv2.drawChessboardCorners(dbg_image_chess, (6, 9), corners, found);
```

5. Load the test image with a circle grid pattern:

```
image_circles = cv2.imread('../data/circlesgrid.png')
```

6. Detect the circle grid pattern:

```
found, corners = cv2.findCirclesGrid(image_circles, (6, 6),
cv2.CALIB_CB_SYMMETRIC_GRID)
assert found == True, "can't find circles grid pattern"
```

7. Draw the detected pattern:

```
dbg_image_circles = image_circles.copy()
cv2.drawChessboardCorners(dbg_image_circles, (6, 6), corners,
found);
```

8. Visualize the results:

```
plt.figure(figsize=(8,8))
plt.subplot(221)
plt.title('original')
plt.axis('off')
plt.imshow(image_chess)
plt.subplot(222)
plt.title('detected pattern')
plt.axis('off')
plt.imshow(dbg_image_chess)
plt.show()
plt.subplot(223)
plt.title('original')
plt.axis('off')
plt.imshow(image_circles)
plt.subplot(224)
```

```
plt.title('detected pattern')
plt.axis('off')
plt.imshow(dbg_image_circles)
plt.tight_layout()
plt.show()
```

How it works...

Calibration pattern detection is implemented with two OpenCV functions: `cv2.findChessboardCorners` and `cv2.findCirclesGrid`. Both functions return Boolean flags indicating whether the pattern is found or not, and the corner points, if found.

The following output is expected:

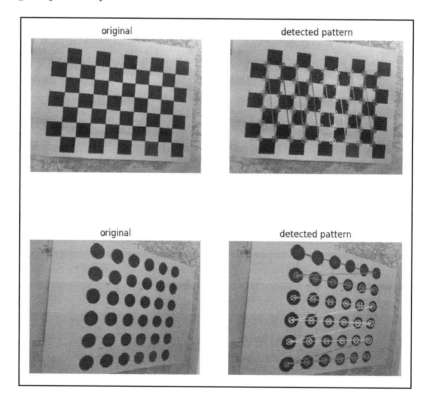

A simple pedestrian detector using the SVM model

In this recipe, you will learn how to detect pedestrians using a pre-trained SVM model with HOG features. Pedestrian detection is an important component of many **Advanced Driver Assistance Solutions** (**ADAS**). Pedestrian detection is also used in video surveillance systems, and many other computer vision applications.

Getting ready

Before you proceed with this recipe, you need to install the OpenCV 3.x Python API package and the matplotlib package.

How to do it...

1. Import the modules:

```
import cv2
import matplotlib.pyplot as plt
```

2. Load the test image:

```
image = cv2.imread('../data/people.jpg')
```

3. Create the HOG feature computer and detector:

```
hog = cv2.HOGDescriptor()
hog.setSVMDetector(cv2.HOGDescriptor_getDefaultPeopleDetector())
```

4. Detect the people in the image:

```
locations, weights = hog.detectMultiScale(image)
```

5. Draw the detected people bounding boxes:

```
dbg_image = image.copy()
for loc in locations:
    cv2.rectangle(dbg_image, (loc[0], loc[1]),
                  (loc[0]+loc[2], loc[1]+loc[3]), (0, 255, 0), 2)
```

6. Visualize the results:

```
plt.figure(figsize=(12,6))
plt.subplot(121)
plt.title('original')
plt.axis('off')
plt.imshow(image[:,:,[2,1,0]])
plt.subplot(122)
plt.title('detections')
plt.axis('off')
plt.imshow(dbg_image[:,:,[2,1,0]])
plt.tight_layout()
plt.show()
```

How it works...

OpenCV implements the **Histogram-of-Oriented-Gradients** (**HOG**) descriptor computation functionality in the class `cv2.HOGDescriptor`. The same class can be used for object detection using a linear SVM model. In fact, it already has a pre-trained pedestrian detector model with weights. The model can be obtained through the method `cv2.HOGDescriptor.getDefaultPeopleDetector`. Objects are detected using the sliding window approach at multiple scales, using the method `hog.detectMultiScale`. The function returns a list of locations of detected people, and each detection score. To know more visit `https://en.wikipedia.org/wiki/Histogram_of_oriented_gradients`.

The following output is expected:

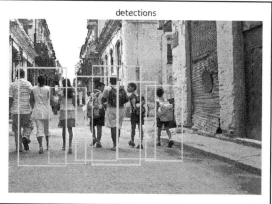

Optical character recognition using different machine learning models

In this recipe, you will learn how to train KNN- and SVM-based digit recognition models. It's a simple **Optical Character Recognition (OCR)** system that can be extended for other characters as well. OCR is a powerful instrument used in many practical applications for recognizing text documents, automatically reading traffic sign messages, and so on.

Getting ready

Before you proceed with this recipe, you will need to install the OpenCV 3.x Python API package and the `matplotlib` package.

How to do it...

1. Import the modules:

    ```
    import cv2
    import numpy as np
    ```

2. Specify a few constants:

    ```
    CELL_SIZE = 20      # Digit image size.
    NCLASSES = 10       # Number of digits.
    TRAIN_RATIO = 0.8   # Part of all samples used for training.
    ```

3. Read the digits image and prepare the labels:

    ```
    digits_img = cv2.imread('../data/digits.png', 0)
    digits = [np.hsplit(r, digits_img.shape[1] // CELL_SIZE)
              for r in np.vsplit(digits_img, digits_img.shape[0] //
    CELL_SIZE)]
    digits = np.array(digits).reshape(-1, CELL_SIZE, CELL_SIZE)
    nsamples = digits.shape[0]
    labels = np.repeat(np.arange(NCLASSES), nsamples // NCLASSES)
    ```

4. Perform geometric normalization, compute image moments, and align each sample:

```
for i in range(nsamples):
    m = cv2.moments(digits[i])
    if m['mu02'] > 1e-3:
        s = m['mu11'] / m['mu02']
        M = np.float32([[1, -s, 0.5*CELL_SIZE*s],
                        [0, 1, 0]])
        digits[i] = cv2.warpAffine(digits[i], M, (CELL_SIZE,
CELL_SIZE))
```

5. Shuffle the samples:

```
perm = np.random.permutation(nsamples)
digits = digits[perm]
labels = labels[perm]
```

6. Define a function for computing HOG descriptors:

```
def calc_hog(digits):
    win_size = (20, 20)
    block_size = (10, 10)
    block_stride = (10, 10)
    cell_size = (10, 10)
    nbins = 9
    hog = cv2.HOGDescriptor(win_size, block_size, block_stride,
cell_size, nbins)
    samples = []
    for d in digits: samples.append(hog.compute(d))
    return np.array(samples, np.float32)
```

7. Prepare the train and test data (features and labels):

```
ntrain = int(TRAIN_RATIO * nsamples)
fea_hog_train = calc_hog(digits[:ntrain])
fea_hog_test = calc_hog(digits[ntrain:])
labels_train, labels_test = labels[:ntrain], labels[ntrain:]
```

8. Create a KNN model:

```
K = 3
knn_model = cv2.ml.KNearest_create()
knn_model.train(fea_hog_train, cv2.ml.ROW_SAMPLE, labels_train)
```

9. Create an SVM model:

```
svm_model = cv2.ml.SVM_create()
svm_model.setGamma(2)
svm_model.setC(1)
svm_model.setKernel(cv2.ml.SVM_RBF)
svm_model.setType(cv2.ml.SVM_C_SVC)
svm_model.train(fea_hog_train, cv2.ml.ROW_SAMPLE, labels_train)
```

10. Define a function for evaluating the models:

```
def eval_model(fea, labels, fpred):
    pred = fpred(fea).astype(np.int32)
    acc = (pred.T == labels).mean()*100
    conf_mat = np.zeros((NCLASSES, NCLASSES), np.int32)
    for c_gt, c_pred in zip(labels, pred):
        conf_mat[c_gt, c_pred] += 1
    return acc, conf_mat
```

11. Evaluate the KNN and SVM models:

```
knn_acc, knn_conf_mat = eval_model(fea_hog_test, labels_test,
lambda fea: knn_model.findNearest(fea, K)[1])
print('KNN accuracy (%):', knn_acc)
print('KNN confusion matrix:')
print(knn_conf_mat)

svm_acc, svm_conf_mat = eval_model(fea_hog_test, labels_test,
lambda fea: svm_model.predict(fea)[1])
print('SVM accuracy (%):', svm_acc)
print('SVM confusion matrix:')
print(svm_conf_mat)
```

How it works...

In this recipe, we apply a lot of different OpenCV functions to build an application for recognizing digits. We use `cv2.moment` for estimating image skew, and then normalize it with `cv2.warpAffine`. KNN and SVM models are created with the `cv2.ml.KNearest_create` and `cv2.ml.SVM_create` methods. We randomly shuffle all of the available data, and then split it into train/test subsets. The function `eval_model` computes the overall model accuracy and the confusion matrix. In the results, we can see that the SVM-based model gives slightly better results than the KNN one.

The following output is expected:

```
KNN accuracy (%): 91.1
KNN confusion matrix:
[[101   0   0   0   0   0   1   0   0   2]
 [  0 112   3   0   0   0   0   0   0   0]
 [  0   1  93   1   0   0   0   0   2   0]
 [  1   0   3 100   0   3   0   0   1   1]
 [  1   0   2   8  78   3   4   0   1   5]
 [  0   0   0   5   0  82   1   0   4   1]
 [  0   0   0   0   1   0  92   0   0   0]
 [  0   0   3   6   2   1   0  76   1   2]
 [  0   0   0   1   0   2   0   1  80   2]
 [  2   1   1   1   0   0   0   4   4  97]]

SVM accuracy (%): 93.5
SVM confusion matrix:
[[100   0   1   0   0   0   1   0   0   2]
 [  0 112   2   0   0   0   0   1   0   0]
 [  0   0  93   0   1   0   0   1   2   0]
 [  1   0   2 100   0   2   0   1   2   1]
 [  1   0   1   2  93   2   0   1   0   2]
 [  0   0   0   3   1  85   1   1   2   0]
 [  0   0   0   0   1   0  92   0   0   0]
 [  0   0   1   3   3   2   0  82   0   0]
 [  2   0   0   1   0   2   0   0  79   2]
 [  1   1   1   1   1   1   0   4   1  99]]
```

Confusion matrices show how many, and what kind of mistakes a model makes. Each row corresponds to a ground truth class label, and each column corresponds to a predicted class label. All of the off-diagonal elements are classification errors, while each diagonal element is the number of proper classifications.

Detecting faces using Haar/LBP cascades

How often have you been impressed with your phone or digital camera when faces on the photo have been detected? There's no doubt you want to implement something similar on your own, or incorporate a face detection feature in your algorithms. This recipe shows how you can easily repeat this using OpenCV. Let's get started.

Getting ready

Before you proceed with this recipe, you need to install the OpenCV 3.x Python API package.

How to do it...

The steps for this recipe are:

1. Import the modules we need:

```
import cv2
import numpy as np
```

2. Define the function that opens a video file, invokes a detector to find all of the faces in the image, and displays the results:

```
def detect_faces(video_file, detector, win_title):
    cap = cv2.VideoCapture(video_file)

    while True:
        status_cap, frame = cap.read()
        if not status_cap:
            break

        gray = cv2.cvtColor(frame, cv2.COLOR_BGR2GRAY)

        faces = detector.detectMultiScale(gray, 1.3, 5)

        for x, y, w, h in faces:
            cv2.rectangle(frame, (x, y), (x + w, y + h), (0, 255,
0), 3)
            text_size, _ = cv2.getTextSize('Face',
cv2.FONT_HERSHEY_SIMPLEX, 1, 2)
            cv2.rectangle(frame, (x, y - text_size[1]), (x +
text_size[0], y), (255, 255, 255), cv2.FILLED)
            cv2.putText(frame, 'Face', (x, y),
cv2.FONT_HERSHEY_SIMPLEX, 1, (0, 0, 0), 2)
        cv2.imshow(win_title, frame)

        if cv2.waitKey(1) == 27:
            break

    cv2.destroyAllWindows()
```

3. Load the pre-trained Haar cascade from OpenCV, and call our detect function:

```
haar_face_cascade =
cv2.CascadeClassifier('../data/haarcascade_frontalface_default.xml'
)

detect_faces('../data/faces.mp4', haar_face_cascade, 'Haar cascade
face detector')
```

4. Load the pre-trained LBP cascade in a slightly different manner, and invoke the function again to find and display faces:

```
lbp_face_cascade = cv2.CascadeClassifier()
lbp_face_cascade.load('../data/lbpcascade_frontalface.xml')

detect_faces(0, lbp_face_cascade, 'LBP cascade face detector')
```

How it works...

The object detector is an algorithm that is able to find objects in the image, it computes the parameters of the bounding box inside of which there is an object, and also determines to which category (or class) the object belongs. In this recipe, we're working with detectors for only one category, upright frontal face.

Detectors can be based on various technologies, and usually involve machine learning. This recipe tells you how to use cascade-based detectors. One of the main advantages of this type of detector is its working time, it handles images even faster than real time on modern hardware, and that's why it's still popular.

OpenCV contains a lot of pre-trained detectors for different purposes, you can find bounding boxes for cats, eyes, license plates, bodies, and of course, faces. All of these detectors are available in the main OpenCV repository, in the /data subdirectory (https:/ /github.com/opencv/opencv/tree/master/data). All detectors are represented with .xml files, which contain all of the parameters of the detectors.

To create the detector, you need to use the cv2.CascadeClassifier class constructor. You can pass path to XML file with cascade parameters to the constructor—it load detected from the file then. Also, you can load the parameters later by using the load function, as shown in the preceding code.

To use the loaded classifier, you need to call the `detectMultiScale` function of its instance. It accepts these arguments: the 8-bit grayscale image where you can find the objects, the scale factor, the neighbors number, flags, and the minimal and maximal object sizes. The scale factor determines how we scale an image to find objects at different sizes; bigger values lead to faster computation, but also to a higher probability of rejecting faces of intermediate sizes. The neighbors number calls to increase the robustness of the algorithm, this number determines how many overlapped detections there should be for the current object to count it as a true object. Flags are used for previously created classifiers, and are necessary for backward compatibility. Minimal and maximal sizes are obviously determined boundaries for the object sizes we want to detect. `detectMultiScale` returns a list of bounding boxes for objects in the input image; each box is in an (*x*, *y*, width, height) format.

As a result of launching the code, you will see an image like the following:

 If you're interested in training your own cascade classifier, OpenCV has a good tutorial on this topic. The tutorial can be found at `https://docs.opencv.org/3.3.0/dc/d88/tutorial_traincascade.html`.

Detecting AruCo patterns for AR applications

Understanding a camera's position in a surrounding 3D space is a very challenging and hard-to-solve task. Specifically designed patterns, named AruCo markers, are called up to solve this issue. Each marker has enough information to determine the camera position, and also contains information about itself; so it's possible to distinguish between different markers, and, through that, understand the scene. In this recipe, we will review how to create and detect AruCo markers with OpenCV.

Getting ready

Before you proceed with this recipe, you will need to install the OpenCV 3.x Python API package with the OpenCV contrib modules.

How to do it...

1. Import the modules:

```
import cv2
import cv2.aruco as aruco
import numpy as np
```

2. Create an image with different AruCo markers, blur it, and then display it:

```
aruco_dict = aruco.getPredefinedDictionary(aruco.DICT_6X6_250)

img = np.full((700, 700), 255, np.uint8)

img[100:300, 100:300] = aruco.drawMarker(aruco_dict, 2, 200)
img[100:300, 400:600] = aruco.drawMarker(aruco_dict, 76, 200)
img[400:600, 100:300] = aruco.drawMarker(aruco_dict, 42, 200)
img[400:600, 400:600] = aruco.drawMarker(aruco_dict, 123, 200)

img = cv2.GaussianBlur(img, (11, 11), 0)

cv2.imshow('Created AruCo markers', img)
cv2.waitKey(0)
cv2.destroyAllWindows()
```

3. Detect the markers on the blurred image. Draw the detected markers and display the results:

```
aruco_dict = aruco.getPredefinedDictionary(aruco.DICT_6X6_250)

corners, ids, _ = aruco.detectMarkers(img, aruco_dict)

img_color = cv2.cvtColor(img, cv2.COLOR_GRAY2BGR)
aruco.drawDetectedMarkers(img_color, corners, ids)

cv2.imshow('Detected AruCo markers', img_color)
cv2.waitKey(0)
cv2.destroyAllWindows()
```

How it works...

As has been mentioned, AruCo markers have special designs and encode an identifier in black and white squares inside. So, to create the proper marker, it's necessary to follow the rules, and to also set parameters, such as the marker size and identifier. All of this can be done with the `cv2.aruco.drawMarker` function. It accepts a dictionary of the markers, an identifier of the marker, and image size. The dictionary determines the correspondence between the marker's appearance and the marker's ID, and returns the image with a drawn marker. OpenCV includes predefined dictionaries, which can be retrieved with the `cv2.aruco.getPredefinedDictionary` function (which takes the dictionary name as an argument). In the preceding code, `cv2.aruco.DICT_6X6_250` is used, and this dictionary's name means that the dictionary consists of 6x6 markers (the size of the inside grid of black and white squares), and includes identifiers from 0 to 249.

To detect AruCo markers in the image, you need to use the `cv2.aruco.detectMarkers` routine. This function takes an input image and a dictionary from which it is necessary to find markers. The result of this function's work is a list with four corners for all of the found markers, a list of markers IDs (the order corresponds to the list of the corners), and list of rejected corners, which can be useful for debug purposes.

To easily and quickly draw the results of the detection, it's reasonable to use `cv2.aruco.drawDetectedMarkers`. It accepts an image to draw a list of detected corners and a list of identifiers on.

As a result of the code launch, you will get an image like the following:

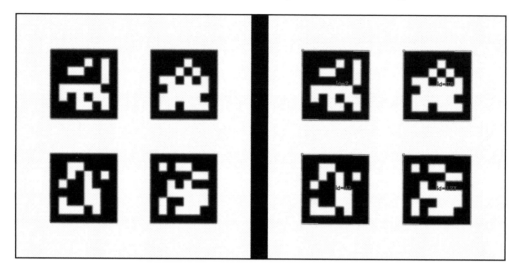

Detecting text in natural scenes

In this recipe, you will learn how to detect text in natural images using a pre-trained convolutional neural network model. Detecting text in natural environments is important in applications like reading traffic sign messages, understanding ad messages, and reading banners.

Getting ready

Before you proceed with this recipe, you will need to install the OpenCV 3.x Python API package and the matplotlib package. OpenCV must be built with contrib modules, because the advanced text recognition functionality isn't a part of the main OpenCV repository.

The modified `.prototxt` file with the model description for this recipe can be found at
`opencv_contrib/modules/text/samples/textbox.prototxt`.

The model weights can be downloaded from `https://www.dropbox.com/s/g8pjzv2de9gty8g/TextBoxes_icdar13.caffemodel?dl=0`.

How to do it...

In order to complete this recipe, you need to perform the following steps:

1. Import the module:

    ```
    import cv2
    ```

2. Load the text image:

    ```
    img = cv2.imread('../data/scenetext01.jpg')
    ```

3. Load the pre-trained convolutional neural network and detect the text messages:

    ```
    det = cv2.text.TextDetectorCNN_create(
            "../data/textbox.prototxt",
    "../data/TextBoxes_icdar13.caffemodel")
    rects, probs = det.detect(img)
    ```

4. Draw the detected text bounding boxes with confidences higher than the threshold:

    ```
    THR = 0.3
    for i, r in enumerate(rects):
        if probs[i] > THR:
            cv2.rectangle(img, (r[0], r[1]), (r[0]+r[2], r[1]+r[3]),
    (0, 255, 0), 2)
    ```

5. Visualize the results:

    ```
    plt.figure(figsize=(10,8))
    plt.axis('off')
    plt.imshow(img[:,:,[2,1,0]])
    plt.tight_layout()
    plt.show()
    ```

How it works...

There are many different text detection methods implemented in OpenCV. In this recipe, you learned how to use a state-of-the-art deep learning approach for detecting text bounding boxes. The OpenCV class `cv2.TextDetectorCNN_create` creates a CNN (convolutional neural network) model, and loads its pre-trained weights from a specified file. After that, you only need to call the `det.detect` method, which returns a list of rectangles with the associated probabilities of rectangles containing text.

The following output is expected:

QR code detector

QR codes, like AruCo markers, are another type of specifically designed object, used to store information and describe 3D space. You can find QR codes almost everywhere, from food packages to museums and robotized factories.

In this recipe, we will understand how to detect QR codes and remove perspective distortions to get a canonical view of the codes. This task may sound easy to complete, but it requires a lot of OpenCV functionality. Let's find out how to do it.

Getting ready

Before you proceed with this recipe, you will need to install the OpenCV 3.x Python API package.

How to do it...

1. Import the modules we need:

```
import cv2
import numpy as np
```

2. Implement a function which finds the intersection point of two lines:

```
def intersect(l1, l2):
    delta = np.array([l1[1] - l1[0], l2[1] -
l2[0]]).astype(np.float32)
    delta = 1 / delta
    delta[:, 0] *= -1
    b = np.matmul(delta, np.array([l1[0], l2[0]]).transpose())
    b = np.diagonal(b).astype(np.float32)
    res = cv2.solve(delta, b)
    return res[0], tuple(res[1].astype(np.int32).reshape((2)))
```

3. Define a function which un-warps the perspective distortions by calculating the correspondence between four pairs of distorted and un-distorted points:

```
def rectify(image, corners, out_size):
    rect = np.zeros((4, 2), dtype = "float32")
    rect[0] = corners[0]
    rect[1] = corners[1]
    rect[2] = corners[2]
    rect[3] = corners[3]

    dst = np.array([
        [0, 0],
        [out_size[1] - 1, 0],
        [out_size[1] - 1, out_size[0] - 1],
        [0, out_size[0] - 1]], dtype = "float32")

    M = cv2.getPerspectiveTransform(rect, dst)
    rectified = cv2.warpPerspective(image, M, out_size)
    return rectified
```

4. Create a function which finds the outer corners of the QR code:

```python
def qr_code_outer_corners(image):
    outer_corners_found = False
    outer_corners = []
    gray = cv2.cvtColor(image, cv2.COLOR_BGR2GRAY)
    _, th = cv2.threshold(gray, 0, 255, cv2.THRESH_BINARY +
cv2.THRESH_OTSU)
    _, contours, hierarchy = \
            cv2.findContours(th, cv2.RETR_TREE,
cv2.CHAIN_APPROX_SIMPLE)
    cnts = []
    centers = []
    hierarchy = hierarchy.reshape((-1, 4))
    for i in range(hierarchy.shape[0]):
        i_next, i_prev, i_child, i_par = hierarchy[i]
        if all(v == -1 for v in hierarchy[i][:3]):
            if all(v == -1 for v in hierarchy[i_par][:2]):
                ids = [i, i_par, hierarchy[i_par][3]]
                corner_cnts = []
                for id_ in ids:
                    cnt = contours[id_]
                    apprx = \
                        cv2.approxPolyDP(cnt, cv2.arcLength(cnt,
True) * 0.02, True)
                    if len(apprx) == 4:
                        corner_cnts.append(apprx.reshape((4, -1)))
                if len(corner_cnts) == 3:
                    cnts.append(corner_cnts)
                    all_pts = np.array(corner_cnts).reshape(-1, 2)
                    centers.append(np.mean(all_pts, 0))
    if len(centers) == 3:
        distances_between_pts = np.linalg.norm(np.roll(centers, 1,
0) - centers, axis=1)
        max_dist_id = np.argmax(distances_between_pts)
        index_diag_pt_1 = max_dist_id
        index_diag_pt_2 = (max_dist_id - 1) % len(centers)
        index_corner_pt = (len(centers) - 1)*len(centers) // 2 -
index_diag_pt_1 - index_diag_pt_2
        middle_pt = 0.5 * (centers[index_diag_pt_1] +
centers[index_diag_pt_2])
        i_ul_pt = \
np.argmax(np.linalg.norm(cnts[index_corner_pt][-1] - middle_pt,
axis=1))
        ul_pt = cnts[index_corner_pt][-1][i_ul_pt]
        for i in [index_diag_pt_1, index_diag_pt_2]:
            corner_cnts = cnts[i]
```

```
            outer_cnt = corner_cnts[-1]
            distances_to_mp = np.linalg.norm(outer_cnt - middle_pt,
    axis=1)
            max_dist_id = np.argmax(distances_to_mp)
            vec_from_mid_to_diag = outer_cnt[max_dist_id] -
    middle_pt
            vec_from_mid_to_corner = ul_pt - middle_pt
            cross_prod = np.cross(vec_from_mid_to_corner,
    vec_from_mid_to_diag)
            diff_idx = 0
            if cross_prod > 0:
                ur_pt = outer_cnt[max_dist_id]
                ur_pt_2 = outer_cnt[(max_dist_id + 1) %
    len(outer_cnt)]
            else:
                bl_pt = outer_cnt[max_dist_id]
                bl_pt_2 = outer_cnt[(max_dist_id - 1) %
    len(outer_cnt)]
        ret, br_pt = intersect((bl_pt, bl_pt_2), (ur_pt, ur_pt_2))
        if ret == True:
            outer_corners_found = True
            outer_corners = [ul_pt, ur_pt, br_pt, bl_pt]
    return outer_corners_found, outer_corners
```

5. Open a video with a QR code, find the QR code on each frame, and, if successful, show the code corners and un-warp the code to get a canonical view:

```
cap = cv2.VideoCapture('../data/qr.mp4')

while True:
    ret, frame = cap.read()
    if ret == False:
        break
    result, corners = qr_code_outer_corners(frame)
    qr_code_size = 300
    if result:
        if all((0, 0) < tuple(c) < (frame.shape[1], frame.shape[0])
for c in corners):
            rectified = rectify(frame, corners, (qr_code_size,
qr_code_size))
            cv2.circle(frame, tuple(corners[0]), 15, (0, 255, 0),
2)
            cv2.circle(frame, tuple(corners[1]), 15, (0, 0, 255),
2)
            cv2.circle(frame, tuple(corners[2]), 15, (255, 0, 0),
2)
            cv2.circle(frame, tuple(corners[3]), 15, (255, 255, 0),
```

```
2)
            frame[0:qr_code_size, 0:qr_code_size] = rectified

    cv2.imshow('QR code detection', frame)
    k = cv2.waitKey(100)
    if k == 27:
        break

cap.release()
cv2.destroyAllWindows()
```

How it works...

If you look at any QR code, you'll see that it has special markers on each of its corners. These markers are just white and black squares inside of each other. So, to detect and localize the QR code, we need to detect these three special markers. We can do that with `cv2.findContours`. We need to exploit the information inside of the central black square; there are no other objects, and consequently, no other contours. The next white square contains only one contour. And again, the next black square contains only two contours. You may remember that `cv2.findContours` can return a hierarchy of contours on the image. We just need to find the described structure of the nested contours. Also, our markers have square shapes, and we can use this information to further exclude false positives. We can approximate our contours with a fewer number of points with the `cv2.approxPolyDP` function. Our contours can be approximated with a four vertex polygon with high accuracy.

After we've found the markers and their contours, we should decide their mutual location. In other words, we should find out whether there are bottom-left and upper-right markers, and whether there is an upper-left one. Bottom-left and upper-right markers lie on the diagonal, so they have the largest distance between them. Using this fact, we can choose the diagonal markers and the upper-left one. Then, we need to figure out which of our diagonal markers is bottom-left. To do this, we find the middle point of the QR code, and see what rotation (clockwise or counter-clockwise) we should perform to match a vector from the middle point to the upper-left corner and a vector from the middle point to one of the diagonal markers. This can be done by finding a sign of a Z projection of the cross product of the vectors.

Now we know all about the three marked corners, and we need to find the last corner of the QR code. To do it, we find an intersection between the lines formed by the sides of the outer squares of diagonal markers. These facts give us two linear equations, with two variables, the x and y coordinates of the intersection point. `cv2.solve` can tackle this issue and find the solution of our linear system.

At this point, we have all four outer corners of the QR code, and we need to eliminate perspective transformations and get a canonical view of the code. This can be done by applying `cv2.warpPerspective`.

After launching the code, you will get something similar to the following image:

5

Deep Learning

This chapter contains recipes for:

- Representing images as tensors/blobs
- Loading Deep Learning models from Caffe, Torch, and TensorFlow formats
- Getting input and output tensors' shapes for all layers
- Preprocessing images and inference in convolutional networks
- Measuring inference time and contributions to it from each layer
- Classifying images with GoogleNet/Inception and ResNet models
- Detecting objects with the Single Shot Detection (SSD) model
- Segmenting a scene using the Fully Convolutional Network (FCN) model
- Face detection using Single Shot Detection (SSD) and the ResNet model
- Prediction age and gender

Introduction

Everything is better with Deep Learning. Or is it? It seems that time will tell. But one undoubtable fact is that more and more issues can be solved with deep learning models. Deep Learning now plays an important role in many sciences, and computer vision isn't an exception. OpenCV has recently acquired the ability of loading and inferencing trained models from three popular frameworks: `Caffe`, `Torch`, and `Tensorflow`. This chapter tells you how to work with this functionality of OpenCV. This chapter also contains several useful practical applications of different existing models of classification, semantic segmentation, object detection, and other problems.

Representing images as tensors/blobs

Deep Learning models for computer vision usually get images as an input. However, they do not operate with images, but with tensors. A tensor is more general than an image; it's not limited by two-spatial and one-channel dimensions. In this recipe, we will learn how to convert an image to a multidimensional tensor.

Getting ready

Before you proceed with this recipe, you need to install the OpenCV 3.3 (or greater) Python API package.

How to do it...

You need to complete the following steps:

1. Import the modules:

   ```
   import cv2
   import numpy as np
   ```

2. Open an input image and print its shape:

   ```
   image_bgr = cv2.imread('../data/Lena.png', cv2.IMREAD_COLOR)
   print(image_bgr.shape)
   ```

3. Transform the image to a four-dimensional floating point tensor:

   ```
   image_bgr_float = image_bgr.astype(np.float32)
   image_rgb = image_bgr_float[..., ::-1]
   tensor_chw = np.transpose(image_rgb, (2, 0, 1))
   tensor_nchw = tensor_chw[np.newaxis, ...]

   print(tensor_nchw.shape)
   ```

How it works...

As you know, matrices and images in the OpenCV Python package are presented with NumPy arrays. For example, `cv2.imread` in the previous code gives a colorful image, which is a three-dimensional array, where all three dimensions correspond to height, width, and channels, respectively. It can be imagined as a two-dimensional matrix with height by width elements, and each element stores three values for each red, green, and blue channel. This order of dimensions can be encoded as the letters **height, width, and channels (HWC)**, and data along the channels dimension is stored in the order blue, green, red.

Tensors are multidimensional matrices. Many Deep Learning models accept four-dimensional floating point tensors three for height, width, and channels; and an extra one. Usually the models process not one image but many in a single pass. This bunch of images is called a batch and the fourth dimension addresses individual images in the batch.

The OpenCV Deep Learning functionality operates four-dimensional floating-point tensors with an NCHW order of dimensions: N for the number of images in the batch, C for the number of channels, and H and W are for the height and width, respectively.

So, to turn an image into a tensor, we need to perform the following steps:

1. Convert the image to a floating-point
2. Change the BGR order of channels to RGB if necessary
3. Turn the HWC image to a CHW tensor
4. Add a new dimension into the CHW tensor to make it an NCHW one

As you can see, it's easy. But each step is very important and omitting only one can result in many hours of debugging, where you're trying to understand and locate a mistake. For example, why and when do we need to reorder BGR images? The answer is connected with the order of channels which has been used during the model training. If the model is used to handle RGB images, it is highly likely it will perform poorly on BGR images. This small missed detail may cost you a lot of your time.

Loading deep learning models from Caffe, Torch, and TensorFlow formats

One of the great features of OpenCV's dnn module is being able to load trained models from three very popular frameworks: Caffe, Torch, and TensorFlow. Not only does it makes the dnn module very useful, but also it opens up the possibility of combining models from different frameworks into a single pipeline. In this recipe, we will learn how to work with networks from these three frameworks.

Getting ready

Before you proceed with this recipe, you need to install the OpenCV 3.3.1 (or higher) Python API package.

How to do it...

Go through the following steps:

1. Import the modules:

```
import cv2
import numpy as np
```

2. Load a Caffe model:

```
net_caffe =
cv2.dnn.readNetFromCaffe('../data/bvlc_googlenet.prototxt',
'../data/bvlc_googlenet.caffemodel')
```

3. Load a model from Torch:

```
net_torch =
cv2.dnn.readNetFromTorch('../data/torch_enet_model.net')
```

4. Read and parse a TensorFlow trained model:

```
net_tensorflow =
cv2.dnn.readNetFromTensorflow('../data/tensorflow_inception_graph.p
b')
```

How it works...

To load pre-trained models from the frameworks, you need to use the `readNetFromCaffe`, `readNetFromTorch`, or `readNetFromTensorflow` functions for the `Caffe`, `Torch`, and `TensorFlow` networks respectively. All these functions return the `cv2.dnn_Net` object, which is the parsed version of the graph from the model's file.

It's worth mentioning that you may face issues while loading models with complicated architectures or models not having widely spread layers (for example, models with new types of layers, recently added or developed and implemented by you). OpenCV's `dnn` module is still developing and may not include the latest features from Deep Learning frameworks. But despite that fact, the `dnn` module has a lot of supported layer types to load the models that address complicated tasks, and that's what we'll try in further recipes in this chapter.

Where to find pre-trained deep learning models? There are special webpages where you can find the pre-trained model itself, and also useful information about the process of training. For historical reasons these lists of models are called **Model Zoo**. There is such a list for models created in a `Caffe` framework: `https://github.com/BVLC/caffe/wiki/Model-Zoo`; `Tensorflow` models can be found here: `https://github.com/tensorflow/models`.

Getting input and output tensors' shapes for all layers

Sometimes it's necessary to get information about what's going on with the data shape during a forward pass in deep neural networks. For example, some models allow the usage of various input spatial size and, in that case, you may want to know the output tensors' shapes. OpenCV has an option to get all shapes for all tensors (including intermediate tensors) without inference. This recipe reviews ways of using such functionality along with other useful routines relevant to neural nets.

Getting ready

Before you proceed with this recipe, you need to install the OpenCV 3.3.1 (or higher) Python API package.

How to do it...

You need to complete the following steps:

1. Import the modules:

```
import cv2
import numpy as np
```

2. Load a model from `Caffe` and print the information about the types of layers used in the model:

```
net = cv2.dnn.readNetFromCaffe('../data/bvlc_googlenet.prototxt',
                               '../data/bvlc_googlenet.caffemodel')

if not net.empty():
    print('Net loaded successfully\n')
print('Net contains:')
for t in net.getLayerTypes():
    print('\t%d layers of type %s' % (net.getLayersCount(t), t))
```

3. Get the tensor shapes for the loaded model and specified input shape. Then print all of the information:

```
layers_ids, in_shapes, out_shapes = net.getLayersShapes([1, 3, 224,
224])

layers_names = net.getLayerNames()

print('Net layers shapes:')
for l in range(len(layers_names)):
    in_num, out_num = len(in_shapes[l]), len(out_shapes[l])
    print('Layer "%s" has %d input(s) and %d output(s)'
          % (layers_names[l], in_num, out_num))
    for i in range(in_num):
        print('\tinput #%d has shape' % i,
in_shapes[l][i].flatten())
    for i in range(out_num):
        print('\toutput #%d has shape' % i,
out_shapes[l][i].flatten())
```

How it works...

The getLayersShapes function of the Net class from the cv2.dnn module computes all tensor shapes. It accepts shape as input, a list of four integers. The elements in the list are the number of examples, number of channels, width, and height of the input tensor. The function returns a tuple of three elements: a list of layer identifiers in the model, a list of input tensor shapes for each layer, and a list of output tensor shapes also for each layer. The list of layer identifiers is necessary when we want to get some additional information about the layers, because some functions of cv2.dnn_Net accept identifiers from this list. Returned lists for the input and output shapes contain all the shapes for all of the outputs of the layers. Since each layer can have several inputs and outputs, these returned lists contain lists of NumPy integer arrays of length 4.

Also, we've used some other functions in the previous code. Let's discuss them too. The empty function of cv2.dnn_Net returns True if the network doesn't contain any layers; it can be used to check whether the model was loaded or not.

The getLayerTypes function returns all layer types that are used in the model. This information can help you to get a basic idea about the model. The getLayersCount function gets the layer type and returns a number of layers with specified type. The getLayerNames function gives you all of the names for the layers in the model. Basically, neural net models contain names for the layers and they are preserved during loading and parsing. These names are returned by the getLayerNames function.

Preprocessing images and inference in convolutional networks

We train artificial neural networks for application in our tasks. Here, some conditions arise. Firstly, we need to prepare input data in the format and range that our network can handle. Secondly, we need to pass our data to the network properly. OpenCV helps us to perform both steps, and in this recipe we examine how to use OpenCV's dnn module to easily convert an image to a tensor and perform an inference.

Getting ready

Before you proceed with this recipe, you need to install the OpenCV 3.3.1 (or higher) Python API package.

How to do it...

For this recipe, you need to complete the following steps:

1. Import the modules we're going to use:

```
import cv2
import numpy as np
```

2. Open an input image, preprocess it, and convert it to a tensor:

```
image = cv2.imread('../data/Lena.png', cv2.IMREAD_COLOR)
tensor = cv2.dnn.blobFromImage(image, 1.0, (224, 224),
                               (104, 117, 123), False, False);
```

3. Convert two images to tensors with preliminary preprocessing:

```
tensor = cv2.dnn.blobFromImages([image, image], 1.0, (224, 224),
                                (104, 117, 123), False, True);
```

4. Load a trained neural network model:

```
net = cv2.dnn.readNetFromCaffe('../data/bvlc_googlenet.prototxt',
                               '../data/bvlc_googlenet.caffemodel')
```

5. Set an input for the loaded model and perform an inference:

```
net.setInput(tensor);
prob = net.forward();
```

6. Repeat setting the input and performing the inference with the names of layers specified:

```
net.setInput(tensor, 'data');
prob = net.forward('prob');
```

How it works...

The OpenCV `dnn` module contains a convenient function to convert an image to a tensor with preprocessing, `blobFromImage`. The arguments of this function are the input image (with one or three channels), scale values factor, output spatial size in (width, height) format, mean value to subtract, Boolean flag for whether to swap red and blue channels, and Boolean flag for whether to crop an image from the center before resizing to save the aspect ratio of the object in the image or just resize without preserving the object's proportions. The `blobFromImage` function goes through the following steps while converting an image to a tensor:

1. The function resizes the image. If the crop flag is True, the input image is resized while preserving the aspect ratio. One dimension (width or height) of the image is set to a desirable value and the other is set equal or greater than the corresponding value in the size argument. Then, the resulting image from the center is cropped to the necessary size. If the crop flag is `False`, the function just resizes to the target spatial size.
2. The function converts the values of the resized image to a floating-point type, if necessary.
3. The function swaps the first and last channels if the corresponding argument is True. This is necessary because OpenCV gives images in the BGR channel order after loading, but some Deep Learning models may be trained for images with the RGB channel order.
4. The function then subtracts the mean value from each pixel of the image. The corresponding argument may be either a three-value tuple or just a one-value tuple. If it is a three-value tuple, each value is subtracted from the corresponding channel after the channels are swapped. If it's a single value, it is subtracted from each channel.
5. Multiply the resulting image by the scale factor (2nd argument).
6. Convert the three-dimensional image to a four-dimensional tensor with an NCHW order of dimensions.

The `blobFromImage` function returns a four-dimensional floating-point tensor with all of the preprocessing performed.

It's important to say that the preprocessing must be the same as it was while training the model. Otherwise, the model may work poorly or even not work at all. If you've trained the model yourself, you know all the parameters. But if you've found the model on the internet, you need to examine the description of the model or training scripts to get the necessary information.

If you want to create a tensor from several images, you need to use the `blobFromImages` routine. It has the same arguments as the previous function except the first one, the first argument should be a list of images from which you want to create tensors. The images are converted into tensors in the same order as they are listed in the first argument.

To make an inference, you have to set a tensor as an input of the model with `cv2.dnn_Net.setInput` and then call `cv2.dnn_Net.forward` to get the network's output. `setInput` accepts a tensor that you want to be set, and optionally the name of the input. When the model has several inputs, the name of the input determines which one we want to set.

The `forward` function performs all computations from input to output, layer by layer, and returns the resulting tensor. Also, you can specify the output of which layer you need to be returned by passing a name of the layer as an argument.

One question arises, how to interpret the output of the model? The interpretation depends on the model itself. It maybe probabilities of classes for input image, segmentation maps or some more complicated structures. The only way to know exactly is to check out the information about the model's architecture and training procedure.

Measuring inference time and contributions to it from each layer

In this recipe, you will learn how to compute the total number of floating point operations in a network performed in forward pass, as well as the amount of memory consumed. This is useful when you want to understand the limitations of your model and reveal where exactly the bottlenecks are so that you can optimize it.

Getting ready

Before you proceed with this recipe, you need to install OpenCV 3.x with Python API support.

How to do it...

You need to perform the following steps:

1. Import the modules:

```
import cv2
import numpy as np
```

2. Import the `Caffe` model:

```
model = cv2.dnn.readNetFromCaffe('../data/bvlc_googlenet.prototxt',
'../data/bvlc_googlenet.caffemodel')
```

3. Compute the number of FLOPs performed in the inference stage:

```
print('gflops:', model.getFLOPS((1,3,224,224))*1e-9)
```

4. Report the amount of memory consumed for storing weights and intermediate tensors:

```
w,b = model.getMemoryConsumption((1,3,224,224))
print('weights (mb):', w*1e-6, ', blobs (mb):', b*1e-6)
```

5. Perform a forward pass for a mock input:

```
blob = cv2.dnn.blobFromImage(np.zeros((224,224,3), np.uint8), 1,
(224,224))
model.setInput(blob)
model.forward()
```

6. Report the total time:

```
total,timings = model.getPerfProfile()
tick2ms = 1e3/cv2.getTickFrequency()
print('inference (ms): {:2f}'.format(total*tick2ms))
```

7. Report the per layer inference time:

```
layer_names = model.getLayerNames()
print('{: <30} {}'.format('LAYER', 'TIME (ms)'))
for (i,t) in enumerate(timings):
    print('{: <30} {:.2f}'.format(layer_names[i], t[0]*tick2ms))
```

How it works...

You can obtain the model FLOPs count and the amount of memory consumed using the `model.getFLOPs` and `model.getMemoryConsumption` methods. Both methods take as input the specified blob shape. Per-layer inference time statistics are available after the forward pass is performed and can be obtained via the `model.getPerfProfile` method, which returns total inference time and per-layer timings, all in ticks.

The following output is expected:

```
gflops: 3.1904431360000003
weights (mb): 27.994208 , blobs (mb): 45.92096
inference (ms): 83.478832
LAYER TIME (ms)
conv1/7x7_s2 4.57
conv1/relu_7x7 0.00
pool1/3x3_s2 0.74
pool1/norm1 1.49
conv2/3x3_reduce 0.57
conv2/relu_3x3_reduce 0.00
conv2/3x3 11.53
conv2/relu_3x3 0.00
conv2/norm2 3.35
pool2/3x3_s2 0.90
inception_3a/1x1 0.55
...
inception_5b/relu_pool_proj 0.00
inception_5b/output 0.00
pool5/7x7_s1 0.07
pool5/drop_7x7_s1 0.00
loss3/classifier 0.30
prob 0.02
```

Classifying images with GoogleNet/Inception and ResNet models

In computer vision, a classification task is the estimation of the probability that an input image belongs to a particular category. In other words, the algorithm must determine the category for the image and the main goal is to create a classifier with the lowest number of errors. Classification tasks first gave deep learning algorithms an edge over other algorithms. Since then, Deep Learning has gained huge interest from many scientists and engineers. In this recipe, we will apply three models with different architectures to the classification task.

Getting ready

Before you proceed with this recipe, you need to install the OpenCV 3.3.1 Python API package.

How to do it...

You need to follow these steps:

1. Import the modules:

```
import cv2
import numpy as np
```

2. Define a `classify` function, which gets frames from the video, transforms them into tensors, feeds them to the neural network, and selects five categories with the highest probability:

```
def classify(video_src, net, in_layer, out_layer,
             mean_val, category_names, swap_channels=False):
    cap = cv2.VideoCapture(video_src)

    t = 0
    while True:
        status_cap, frame = cap.read()
        if not status_cap:
            break

        if isinstance(mean_val, np.ndarray):
            tensor = cv2.dnn.blobFromImage(frame, 1.0, (224, 224),
```

```
                      1.0, False);
           tensor -= mean_val
       else:
           tensor = cv2.dnn.blobFromImage(frame, 1.0, (224, 224),
                                 mean_val, swap_channels);
       net.setInput(tensor, in_layer);
       prob = net.forward(out_layer);

       prob = prob.flatten()

       r = 1
       for i in np.argsort(prob)[-5:]:
           txt = '"%s"; probability: %.2f' % (category_names[i],
prob[i])
           cv2.putText(frame, txt, (0, frame.shape[0] - r*40),
                       cv2.FONT_HERSHEY_SIMPLEX, 1, (0, 255, 0),
2);
           r += 1

       cv2.imshow('classification', frame)
       if cv2.waitKey(1) == 27:
           break
   cv2.destroyAllWindows()
   cap.release()
```

3. Open a file with names for the categories:

```
with open('../data/synset_words.txt') as f:
    class_names = [' '.join(l.split(' ')[1:]).rstrip() for l in
f.readlines()]
```

4. Load a `GoogleNet` model from `Caffe` and invoke our `classify` function, defined earlier in *Step 2*:

```
googlenet_caffe =
cv2.dnn.readNetFromCaffe('../data/bvlc_googlenet.prototxt',
'../data/bvlc_googlenet.caffemodel')

classify('../data/shuttle.mp4', googlenet_caffe, 'data', 'prob',
(104, 117, 123), class_names)
```

5. Open a ResNet-50 model again from `Caffe`, load a tensor with mean values, and again call `classify`:

```
resnet_caffe =
cv2.dnn.readNetFromCaffe('../data/resnet_50.prototxt',
'../data/resnet_50.caffemodel')
mean = np.load('../data/resnet_50_mean.npy')

classify('../data/shuttle.mp4', resnet_caffe, 'data', 'prob', mean,
class_names)
```

6. Load the category names with which a `GoogleNet` model from `TensorFlow` has been trained, load this model from `TensorFlow`, and classify the frames from the video:

```
with open('../data/imagenet_comp_graph_label_strings.txt') as f:
    class_names = [l.rstrip() for l in f.readlines()]

googlenet_tf =
cv2.dnn.readNetFromTensorflow('../data/tensorflow_inception_graph.p
b')

classify('../data/shuttle.mp4', googlenet_tf,
         'input', 'softmax2', 117, class_names, True)
```

How it works...

Neural network models for classification usually accept three-channel images and produce a vector with probabilities across categories. To use a trained model, you need to know a few things:

- What preprocessing of input images has been used in training
- Which layers are inputs and which are outputs
- How data is organized in the output tensor
- What meaning the values in the output tensor have

In our case, each model requires its own preprocessing. Also, models need different orders of channels. Without these two things, models won't work as well (sometimes slightly, sometimes dramatically). Also, models have different names for input and output layers.

Output vectors in classification contain probabilities for all categories. Indexes for maximal values in the outputs are indexes for categories. To convert such indexes to names, you need to parse a special file with matches between categories indexes and their names. These files may be (and in our case are) different for different models.

After executing the code, you will get images similar to the following:

Detecting objects with the Single Shot Detection (SSD) model

In this recipe, you will learn how to detect objects using the **Single Shot Detection** (**SSD**) approach with the pretrained MobileNet network. The model supports 20 classes and can be used in many computer vision applications where finding objects in a scene is required, such as vehicle-collision warning. To know more visit https://arxiv.org/abs/1512.02325.

Getting ready

Before you proceed with this recipe, you need to install the OpenCV 3.x Python API package.

How to do it...

You need to complete these steps:

1. Import the modules:

   ```
   import cv2
   import numpy as np
   ```

2. Import the Caffe model:

   ```
   model =
   cv2.dnn.readNetFromCaffe('../data/MobileNetSSD_deploy.prototxt',
   '../data/MobileNetSSD_deploy.caffemodel')
   ```

3. Set a confidence threshold and specify the classes supported by the model:

   ```
   CONF_THR = 0.3
   LABELS = {1: 'aeroplane', 2: 'bicycle', 3: 'bird', 4: 'boat',
             5: 'bottle', 6: 'bus', 7: 'car', 8: 'cat', 9: 'chair',
             10: 'cow', 11: 'diningtable', 12: 'dog', 13: 'horse',
             14: 'motorbike', 15: 'person', 16: 'pottedplant',
             17: 'sheep', 18: 'sofa', 19: 'train', 20: 'tvmonitor'}
   ```

4. Open the video with road traffic:

```
video = cv2.VideoCapture('../data/traffic.mp4')
while True:
    ret, frame = video.read()
    if not ret: break
```

5. Detect the objects:

```
h, w = frame.shape[0:2]
blob = cv2.dnn.blobFromImage(frame, 1/127.5, (300*w//h,300),
                             (127.5,127.5,127.5), False)
model.setInput(blob)
output = model.forward()
```

6. Draw the detected objects:

```
for i in range(output.shape[2]):
    conf = output[0,0,i,2]
    if conf > CONF_THR:
        label = output[0,0,i,1]
        x0,y0,x1,y1 = (output[0,0,i,3:7] *
[w,h,w,h]).astype(int)
        cv2.rectangle(frame, (x0,y0), (x1,y1), (0,255,0), 2)
        cv2.putText(frame, '{}: {:.2f}'.format(LABELS[label],
conf),
                     (x0,y0), cv2.FONT_HERSHEY_SIMPLEX, 1,
(0,255,0), 2)
    cv2.imshow('frame', frame)
    key = cv2.waitKey(3)
    if key == 27: break
cv2.destroyAllWindows()
```

How it works...

In this recipe, we used the SSD approach for vehicle detection, which uses MobileNet as a backbone network. The model was pretrained by the MS COCO dataset and supports a lot of generic classes, such as person, car, and bird.

In the code, we specified the minimal level of confidence required to consider detection successful (CONF_THR=0.3).

The following output is expected:

Segmenting a scene using the Fully Convolutional Network (FCN) model

In this recipe, you will learn how to perform semantic segmentation of an arbitrary image into 21 classes, such as person, car, and bird. This piece of functionality is useful when an understanding of a scene is required; for example, in augmented reality applications and for driver assistance. To know more visit `https://arxiv.org/abs/1605.06211`.

Getting ready

Before you proceed with this recipe, you need to install the OpenCV 3.x Python API package.

Download model weights from `http://dl.caffe.berkeleyvision.org/fcn8s-heavy-pascal.caffemodel` and save the file into the data folder.

How to do it...

You need to complete these steps:

1. Import the modules:

   ```
   import cv2
   import numpy as np
   ```

2. Import the `Caffe` model:

   ```
   model = cv2.dnn.readNetFromCaffe('../data/fcn8s-heavy-
   pascal.prototxt',
                                    '../data/fcn8s-heavy-
   pascal.caffemodel')
   ```

3. Load the image and perform inference:

   ```
   frame = cv2.imread('../data/scenetext01.jpg')
   blob = cv2.dnn.blobFromImage(frame, 1,
   (frame.shape[1],frame.shape[0]))
   model.setInput(blob)
   output = model.forward()
   ```

4. Compute the image with per-pixel class labels:

   ```
   labels = output[0].argmax(0)
   ```

5. Visualize the results:

   ```
   plt.figure(figsize=(14,10))
   plt.subplot(121)
   plt.axis('off')
   plt.title('original')
   plt.imshow(frame[:,:,[2,1,0]])
   plt.subplot(122)
   plt.axis('off')
   plt.title('segmentation')
   plt.imshow(labels)
   plt.tight_layout()
   plt.show()
   ```

How it works...

We use the VGG-based Fully Convolution Network approach for per-pixel scene segmentation. The model supports 21 classes. The model is quite time consuming and inference might take up a significant amount of CPU time, so be patient.

The following result is expected:

Face detection using Single Shot Detection (SSD) and the ResNet model

In this recipe, you will learn how to detect faces using a convolution neural network model. The ability to accurately detect faces in different conditions is used in various computer vision applications, such as face enhancement.

Getting ready

Before you proceed with this recipe, you need to install the OpenCV 3.x Python API package.

How to do it...

You need to complete these steps:

1. Import the modules:

```
import cv2
import numpy as np
```

2. Load the model and set the confidence threshold:

```
model =
cv2.dnn.readNetFromCaffe('../data/face_detector/deploy.prototxt',
'../data/face_detector/res10_300x300_ssd_iter_140000.caffemodel')
CONF_THR = 0.5
```

3. Open the video:

```
video = cv2.VideoCapture('../data/faces.mp4')
while True:
    ret, frame = video.read()
    if not ret: break
```

4. Detect the faces in the current frame:

```
h, w = frame.shape[0:2]
blob = cv2.dnn.blobFromImage(frame, 1, (300*w//h,300),
(104,177,123), False)
model.setInput(blob)
output = model.forward()
```

5. Visualize the results:

```
for i in range(output.shape[2]):
    conf = output[0,0,i,2]
    if conf > CONF_THR:
        label = output[0,0,i,1]
        x0,y0,x1,y1 = (output[0,0,i,3:7] *
[w,h,w,h]).astype(int)
        cv2.rectangle(frame, (x0,y0), (x1,y1), (0,255,0), 2)
        cv2.putText(frame, 'conf: {:.2f}'.format(conf),
(x0,y0),
                    cv2.FONT_HERSHEY_SIMPLEX, 1, (0,255,0), 2)
    cv2.imshow('frame', frame)
    key = cv2.waitKey(3)
    if key == 27: break
cv2.destroyAllWindows()
```

How it works...

We use the Single Shot Detection approach with the ResNet-10 model. Pay attention to specifying mean color when feeding the input frame.

The following output is expected:

Age and gender prediction

In this recipe, you will learn how to predict a person's age and gender by an image. One of the possible applications is collecting statistical information about people viewing content in digital signage displays for example.

Getting ready

Before you proceed with this recipe, you need to install the OpenCV 3.x Python API package.

How to do it...

You need to complete the following steps:

1. Import the modules:

```
import cv2
import numpy as np
import matplotlib.pyplot as plt
```

2. Load the models:

```
age_model =
cv2.dnn.readNetFromCaffe('../data/age_gender/age_net_deploy.prototx
t',
'../data/age_gender/age_net.caffemodel')
gender_model =
cv2.dnn.readNetFromCaffe('../data/age_gender/gender_net_deploy.prot
otxt',
'../data/age_gender/gender_net.caffemodel')
```

3. Load and crop the source image:

```
orig_frame = cv2.imread('../data/face.jpeg')
dx = (orig_frame.shape[1]-orig_frame.shape[0]) // 2
orig_frame = orig_frame[:,dx:dx+orig_frame.shape[0]]
```

4. Visualize the image:

```
plt.figure(figsize=(6,6))
plt.title('original')
plt.axis('off')
plt.imshow(orig_frame[:,:,[2,1,0]])
plt.show()
```

5. Load the image with mean pixel values and subtract them from the source image:

```
mean_blob = np.load('../data/age_gender/mean.npy')
frame = cv2.resize(orig_frame, (256,256)).astype(np.float32)
frame -= np.transpose(mean_blob[0], (1,2,0))
```

6. Set age and gender lists:

```
AGE_LIST = ['(0, 2)','(4, 6)','(8, 12)','(15, 20)',
            '(25, 32)','(38, 43)','(48, 53)','(60, 100)']
GENDER_LIST = ['male','female']
```

7. Classify gender:

```
blob = cv2.dnn.blobFromImage(frame, 1, (256,256))
gender_model.setInput(blob)
gender_prob = gender_model.forward()
gender_id = np.argmax(gender_prob)
print('Gender: {} with prob: {}'.format(GENDER_LIST[gender_id],
gender_prob[0, gender_id]))
```

8. Classify age group:

```
age_model.setInput(blob)
age_prob = age_model.forward()
age_id = np.argmax(age_prob)
print('Age group: {} with prob: {}'.format(AGE_LIST[age_id],
age_prob[0, age_id]))
```

How it works...

In this recipe, we used two different models: one for gender classification and one for age group classification. Note that in this recipe, in contrast with the others, we subtract per-pixel mean values from the source image, not per-channel values. You can actually visualize the mean values and see the average human face.

Here's the input image:

The following output is expected:

```
Gender: female with prob: 0.9362890720367432
Age group: (25, 32) with prob: 0.9811384081840515
```

6
Linear Algebra

This chapter contains recipes for:

- The orthogonal Procrustes problem
- Rank-constrained matrix approximation
- Principal component analysis
- Solving systems of linear equations (including under- and over-determined)
- Solving polynomial equations
- Linear programming with the simplex method

Introduction

Linear dependence between variables is the simplest of all possible options. It can be found in many applications, from approximation and geometry tasks, to data compression, camera calibration, and machine learning. But despite its simplicity, things get complicated when real-world influences come into play. All data gathered from sensors includes a portion of noise, which can lead systems of linear equations to have unstable solutions. computer vision problems often require solving systems of linear equations. Even in many OpenCV functions, these linear equations are hidden; it's certain that you will face them in your computer vision applications. The recipes in this chapter will acquaint you with approaches from linear algebra that can be useful and actually are used in computer Vision.

The orthogonal Procrustes problem

Originally, this problem questioned ways of finding orthogonal transformation between two matrices. Maybe that doesn't sound relevant to real computer vision applications, but that feeling may change when you consider the fact that a set of points is indeed a matrix. Camera calibration, rigid body transformations, photogrammetry issues, and many other tasks require solving of the orthogonal Procrustes problem. In this recipe, we find a solution to the simple task of estimation point set rotation and examine how our solution is influenced by noisy input data.

Getting ready

Before you proceed with this recipe, you need to install the OpenCV 3.0 (or greater) Python API package.

How to do it...

You need to complete the following steps:

1. Import the modules:

```
import cv2
import numpy as np
```

2. Generate an initial points set. Then create a set of rotated points by applying a rotation matrix to the initial points. Also, add a portion of noise to our rotated points:

```
pts = np.random.multivariate_normal([150, 300], [[1024, 512], [512, 1024]], 50)

rmat = cv2.getRotationMatrix2D((0, 0), 30, 1)[:, :2]
rpts = np.matmul(pts, rmat.transpose())

rpts_noise = rpts + np.random.multivariate_normal([0, 0], [[200, 0], [0, 200]], len(pts))
```

3. Solve the orthogonal Procrustes problem using **Singular Value Decomposition (SVD)** and get an estimate of the rotation matrix:

```
M = np.matmul(pts.transpose(), rpts_noise)

sigma, u, v_t = cv2.SVDecomp(M)

rmat_est = np.matmul(v_t, u).transpose()
```

4. Now we can use the estimated rotation matrix to find out how good our estimation is. To do so, compute the inverted rotation matrix and multiply our previously rotated points by this matrix. Then, calculate the Euclidean distances (L2) between rotated points with and without noise, between rotated back points and initial ones, and also between the original rotation matrix and its estimate:

```
res, rmat_inv = cv2.invert(rmat_est)
assert res != 0
pts_est = np.matmul(rpts, rmat_inv.transpose())

rpts_err = cv2.norm(rpts, rpts_noise, cv2.NORM_L2)
pts_err = cv2.norm(pts_est, pts, cv2.NORM_L2)
rmat_err = cv2.norm(rmat, rmat_est, cv2.NORM_L2)
```

5. Display our data, showing initial points as green-filled circles, rotated points as yellow-filled circles, rotated back points as thin white circles, and rotated points with noise as thin red circles. Then, print the information about L2 differences between the points and matrices and show the resulting image:

```
def draw_pts(image, points, color, thickness=cv2.FILLED):
    for pt in points:
        cv2.circle(img, tuple([int(x) for x in pt]), 10, color,
thickness)

img = np.zeros([512, 512, 3])

draw_pts(img, pts, (0, 255, 0))
draw_pts(img, pts_est, (255, 255, 255), 2)
draw_pts(img, rpts, (0, 255, 255))
draw_pts(img, rpts_noise, (0, 0, 255), 2)

cv2.putText(img, 'R_points L2 diff: %.4f' % rpts_err, (5, 30),
cv2.FONT_HERSHEY_SIMPLEX, 1, (255, 255, 255), 2)
cv2.putText(img, 'Points L2 diff: %.4f' % pts_err, (5, 60),
cv2.FONT_HERSHEY_SIMPLEX, 1, (255, 255, 255), 2)
cv2.putText(img, 'R_matrices L2 diff: %.4f' % rmat_err, (5, 90),
cv2.FONT_HERSHEY_SIMPLEX, 1, (255, 255, 255), 2)
```

```
cv2.imshow('Points', img)
cv2.waitKey()

cv2.destroyAllWindows()
```

How it works...

To find a solution to the orthogonal Procrustes problem, we applied SVD to the multiplication product of two matrices: the matrix composed of initial points and another one composed of points after rotation. The rows in each matrix are (x, y) coordinates of corresponding points. The SVD approach is well-known and gives stability to noise outcomes. `cv2.SVDecomp` is a function that implements SVD in OpenCV. It accepts a matrix (MxN) to decompose and returns three matrices. The first returned matrix is a rectangular diagonal matrix of size MxN, with positive numbers on the diagonal called singular values. The second and third matrices are a left-singular vector matrix and a conjugated transpose of a right-singular vector matrix, respectively.

SVD is an extremely handy tool in linear algebra. It is used a lot in many different tasks because it's able to produce robust solutions. We're not digging deep into the theory of SVD, because it's a separate and indeed vast topic. However, we'll understand this procedure later in other recipes of this chapter.

Let's also review another of OpenCV's functions from the preceding code. The `cv2.getRotationMatrix2D` function hasn't been mentioned previously in this book. It computes a matrix of affine transformation for a given center and angle of rotation and scale. The arguments follow in this order: center of rotation (in (x,y) format), angle of rotation (in degrees), scale. The returned value is a 2x3 matrix of affine transformation.

`cv2.invert` finds a pseudo-inverse matrix for a given one matrix. This function accepts a matrix to invert, and optionally a matrix to save the result and inversion method flag. By default, the flag is set to `cv2.DECOMP_LU`, which applies the LU decomposition to find the result. Also, `cv2.DECOMP_SVD` and `cv2.DECOMP_CHOLESKY` are available as options; the first uses SVD to find a pseudo-inverse matrix (yes, another application of SVD), and the second one applies Cholesky decomposition for the same purpose. The function returns two objects, a `float` value and the resulting inverted matrix. If the first returned value is 0, the input matrix is singular. In this case, `cv2.DECOMP_LU` and `cv2.DECOMP_CHOLESKY` can't produce the result, but `cv2.DECOMP_SVD` computes the pseudo-inverse matrix.

As a result of launching the code from the current recipe, you will get a result similar to the following:

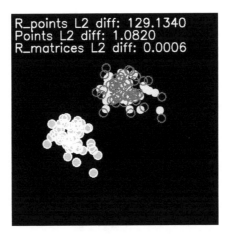

As you can see, despite the fact that the difference between points before and after adding noise is relatively large, the difference between the initial and estimated points and the rotation matrices is slight.

 If you're interested in the theory of the SVD, this Wikipedia page is a good place to start: `https://en.wikipedia.org/wiki/Singular-value_decomposition`.

Rank-constrained matrix approximation

In this recipe, you will learn how to compute a rank-considerant matrix approximation. The problem is formulated as an optimization problem. Given an input matrix, the aim is to find its approximation where the fit is measured using the Frobenius norm and the rank of the output matrix should not be greater than the given value. This functionality, among other fields, is used in data compression and machine learning.

Getting ready

Before you proceed with this recipe, you need to install the OpenCV 3.0 (or greater) Python API package.

How to do it...

You need to complete the following steps:

1. Import the modules:

    ```
    import cv2
    import numpy as np
    ```

2. Generate a random matrix:

    ```
    A = np.random.randn(10, 10)
    ```

3. Compute the SVD:

    ```
    w, u, v_t = cv2.SVDecomp(A)
    ```

4. Compute the rank-constrained matrix approximation:

    ```
    RANK = 5
    w[RANK:,0] = 0
    B = u @ np.diag(w[:,0]) @ v_t
    ```

5. Check the results:

    ```
    print('Rank before:', np.linalg.matrix_rank(A))
    print('Rank after:', np.linalg.matrix_rank(B))
    print('Norm before:', cv2.norm(A))
    print('Norm after:', cv2.norm(B))
    ```

How it works...

The Eckart-Young-Mirsky theorem states that the problem can be solved through computing the SVD (using the `cv2.SVDecomp` function) and constructing an approximation where the smallest singular values are set to zeros, so the approximation rank is not greater than the required value.

Here's what the output should look like:

```
Rank before: 10
Rank after: 5
Norm before: 9.923378133354824
Norm after: 9.511025831320431
```

Principal component analysis

Principal component analysis (PCA) aims to determine the importance of dimensions in data and build up a new basis. In this new basis, directions are selected to have the most independence from others. Because of maximal independence, we can understand which data dimensions carry more information and which carry less. PCA is used in many applications, primarily in data analysis and data compression, but also it can be used in computer vision; for example, to determine and track the orientation of an object. This recipe will show you how to do it in OpenCV.

Getting ready

Before you proceed with this recipe, you need to install the OpenCV 3.0 (or greater) Python API package.

How to do it...

You need to complete the following steps:

1. Import the modules we need:

```
import cv2
import numpy as np
```

2. Define a function that applies PCA to contour points and determines the new basis:

```
def contours_pca(contours):
    # join all contours points into the single matrix and remove
unit dimensions
    cnt_pts = np.vstack(contours).squeeze().astype(np.float32)

    mean, eigvec = cv2.PCACompute(cnt_pts, None)

    center = mean.squeeze().astype(np.int32)
    delta = (150*eigvec).astype(np.int32)
    return center, delta
```

3. Define a function that displays the results of applying PCA to points of contours:

```python
def draw_pca_results(image, contours, center, delta):
    cv2.drawContours(image, contours, -1, (255, 255, 0))

    cv2.line(image, tuple((center + delta[0])),
                    tuple((center - delta[0])),
                    (0, 255, 0), 2)

    cv2.line(image, tuple((center + delta[1])),
                    tuple((center - delta[1])),
                    (0, 0, 255), 2)

    cv2.circle(image, tuple(center), 20, (0, 255, 255), 2)
```

4. Open a video and analyze it frame by frame. For each frame, find contours and apply PCA to the found contours. Then, display the results:

```python
cap = cv2.VideoCapture("../data/opencv_logo.mp4")

while True:
    status_cap, frame = cap.read()
    if not status_cap:
        break
    frame = cv2.resize(frame, (0, 0), frame, 0.5, 0.5)
    edges = cv2.Canny(frame, 250, 150)
    _, contours, _ = cv2.findContours(edges, cv2.RETR_LIST,
cv2.CHAIN_APPROX_SIMPLE)

    if len(contours):
        center, delta = contours_pca(contours)
        draw_pca_results(frame, contours, center, delta)
    cv2.imshow('PCA', frame)
    if cv2.waitKey(100) == 27:
        break

cv2.destroyAllWindows()
```

How it works...

The main idea of tracking object orientation using PCA is that the object doesn't change during rotation. Because it's the same object in different orientations, it has its own basis and this basis rotates together with the object. So, we need to determine this basis in each moment to find an object's orientation. PCA is able to find such basis if we have the right data to analyze. Let's use the points of an object's contours. Of course, they change their absolute position during rotation, but they rotate together with the object. At each orientation, there are directions along which the points of the contours vary the most. And because rotation doesn't skew or distort the contours, these directions are revolved with the object.

`cv2.PCACompute` implements PCA, as the name suggests. It finds eigenvectors and eigenvalues of the data covariance matrix. There are two overloads of this function. The first option, which we use in the preceding code, accepts a matrix of data to analyze, a precomputed mean value, a matrix to write computed eigenvectors, and a number of vectors to return. The last two arguments are optional, and can be omitted (in this case, all vectors are returned). Also, if there is no precomputed mean value, the second parameter can be set to None. In this case, the function computes the mean value as well. The data matrix is usually a set of samples. Each sample has a number of dimensions, D, and there are N samples overall. In this case, the data matrix has to be NxD, and so has N rows, and each row is an individual sample.

As said before, there is a second overload of `cv2.PCACompute`. As previously, it accepts a matrix of data to analyze and a precomputed mean value as the first two arguments. The third and fourth parameters are the ratio of retained variance and the object to store the computed vectors. The ratio determines the number of vectors to return by their variance, the more unbalanced the ratio, the greater the number of retained vectors. This parameter allows you to not fix the number of vectors, but to preserve only the ones with the highest variance.

As a result of the code execution, you will get images similar to the following:

Solving systems of linear equations (including under- and over-determined)

In this recipe, you will learn how to solve systems of linear equations using OpenCV. This functionality is a key building block of many computer vision and machine learning algorithms.

Getting ready

Before you proceed with this recipe, you need to install the OpenCV 3.3 (or greater) Python API package.

How to do it...

You need to complete the following steps:

1. Import the modules:

```
import cv2
import numpy as np
```

2. Generate a system of linear equations:

```
N = 10
A = np.random.randn(N,N)
while np.linalg.matrix_rank(A) < N:
    A = np.random.randn(N,N)
x = np.random.randn(N,1)
b = A @ x
```

3. Solve the system of linear equations:

```
ok, x_est = cv2.solve(A, b)

print('Solved:', ok)
if ok:
    print('Residual:', cv2.norm(b - A @ x_est))
    print('Relative error:', cv2.norm(x_est - x) / cv2.norm(x))
```

4. Construct an over-determined system of linear equations:

```
N = 10
A = np.random.randn(N*2,N)
while np.linalg.matrix_rank(A) < N:
    A = np.random.randn(N*2,N)
x = np.random.randn(N,1)
b = A @ x
```

5. Solve the over-determined system of linear equations:

```
ok, x_est = cv2.solve(A, b, flags=cv2.DECOMP_NORMAL)

print('\nSolved overdetermined system:', ok)
if ok:
    print('Residual:', cv2.norm(b - A @ x_est))
    print('Relative error:', cv2.norm(x_est - x) / cv2.norm(x))
```

6. Construct an under-determined system of linear equations that have more than one solution:

```
N = 10
A = np.random.randn(N,N*2)
x = np.random.randn(N*2,1)
b = A @ x
```

7. Solve the under-determined system of linear equations. Find the solution with minimal norm:

```
w, u, v_t = cv2.SVDecomp(A, flags=cv2.SVD_FULL_UV)
mask = w > 1e-6
w[mask] = 1 / w[mask]
w_pinv = np.zeros((A.shape[1], A.shape[0]))
w_pinv[:N,:N] = np.diag(w[:,0])
A_pinv = v_t.T @ w_pinv @ u.T
x_est = A_pinv @ b

print('\nSolved underdetermined system')
print('Residual:', cv2.norm(b - A @ x_est))
print('Relative error:', cv2.norm(x_est - x) / cv2.norm(x))
```

How it works...

Systems of linear equations can be solved using OpenCV's `cv2.solve` function. It accepts a coefficients matrix, the right-hand side of the system, and optional flags, then returns a solution (the success indicator and solution vector, to be exact). As you can see in the first example, it can be used to solve systems with unique solutions.

You can specify the `cv2.DECOMP_NORMAL` flag, in which case an internally normalized system of linear equations will be constructed. This can be used to solve over-determined systems with one or no solutions, in the latter case, the least squares problem's solution is returned.

An under-determined system of linear equations has either no or multiple solutions. In the preceding code, we constructed a system that has multiple solutions. The solution with minimal norm can be found using the Moore-Penrose inverse (`A_pinv` in the code). As there are multiple solutions, the one we find might have more errors, relative to the solution we used to generate the right-hand side of the system.

Here's an example of the expected output:

```
Solved: True
Residual: 2.7194799110210367e-15
Relative error: 1.1308382847616332e-15

Solved overdetermined system: True
Residual: 4.418021593470969e-15
Relative error: 5.810798787243048e-16

Solved underdetermined system
Residual: 9.296750665059115e-15
Relative error: 0.7288729621745673
```

Solving polynomial equations

In this recipe, you will learn how to solve polynomial equations using OpenCV. Such problems can arise in such areas as machine learning, computational algebra, and signal processing.

Getting ready

Before you proceed with this recipe, you need to install the OpenCV 3.3 (or greater) Python API package.

How to do it...

You need to complete the following steps:

1. Import the modules:

```
import cv2
import numpy as np
```

2. Generate a fourth degree polynomial equation:

```
N = 4
coeffs = np.random.randn(N+1,1)
```

3. Find all the roots in the complex domain:

```
retval, roots = cv2.solvePoly(coeffs)
```

4. Check the roots:

```
for i in range(N):
    print('Root', roots[i],'residual:',
            np.abs(np.polyval(coeffs[::-1],
roots[i][0][0]+1j*roots[i][0][1])))
```

How it works...

Polynomial equations of degree n always have n roots in the complex domain (some of them can be repeated, however). All of the solutions can be found using the `cv2.solvePoly` function. It takes equation coefficients and returns all of the roots.

Here's an example of the expected output:

```
Root [[ 0.0494519    1.12199842]] residual: [  1.50920942e-16]
Root [[-0.17045556  0.         ]] residual: [ 0.]
Root [[ 0.0494519   -1.12199842]] residual: [  1.50920942e-16]
Root [[-8.1939051   0.         ]] residual: [  1.80133686e-14]
```

Linear programming with the simplex method

In this recipe, we consider a special case of optimization problems, problems with linear constraints. These tasks imply that you need to optimize (maximize or minimize) a linear combination of positive variables, taking into account a set of linear constraints. Linear programming doesn't have well-known and direct applications in computer vision, but you may encounter it somewhere down the road. So, let's see how you can deal with linear programming problems using OpenCV.

Getting ready

Before you proceed with this recipe, you need to install the OpenCV 3.0 (or greater) Python API package.

How to do it...

You need to complete the following steps:

1. Import the modules:

```
import cv2
import numpy as np
```

2. Create a linear constraint matrix and weights for the function, which we're going to optimize:

```
m = 10
n = 10
constraints_mat = np.random.randn(m, n+1)
weights = np.random.randn(1, n)
```

3. Apply the simplex method to the task by invoking `cv2.solveLP`. Then, parse the result:

```
solution = np.array((n, 1), np.float32)
res = cv2.solveLP(weights, constrains_mat, solution)

if res == cv2.SOLVELP_SINGLE:
    print('The problem has the one solution')
elif res == cv2.SOLVELP_MULTI:
    print('The problem has the multiple solutions')
elif res == cv2.SOLVELP_UNBOUNDED:
    print('The solution is unbounded')
elif res == cv2.SOLVELP_UNFEASIBLE:
    print('The problem doesnt\'t have any solutions')
```

How it works...

`cv2.solveLP` accepts three arguments: a function's weights, a linear constraints matrix, and a NumPy array object to save results. Weights are represented with an $(N,1)$ or $(1,N)$ vector of float values. The length of this vector also means the number of optimized parameters. The linear constraints matrix is an $(M, N+1)$ NumPy array, where the last column contains constant terms for each constraint and each row, except the last element, which contains coefficients for the corresponding parameters. The last argument is intended to store the solution if it exists.

In general, there are four possible outcomes for linear programming problems, they may have a single solution, many solutions (in some range), or no determined solutions at all. In this latter case, the problem may be unbounded or unfeasible. For all four of these results, `cv2.solveLP` returns a corresponding value: `cv2.SOLVELP_SINGLE`, `cv2.SOLVELP_MULTI`, `cv2.SOLVELP_UNBOUNDED`, or `v2.SOLVELP_UNFEASIBLE`.

7

Detectors and Descriptors

This chapter contains recipes for:

- Finding corners in an image - Harris and FAST
- Selecting good corners in an image for tracking
- Drawing keypoints, descriptors, and matches
- Detecting scale invariant keypoints
- Computing descriptors for image keypoints - SURF, BRIEF, and ORB
- Matching techniques for finding correspondences between descriptors
- Finding reliable matches - cross-check and ratio test
- Model-based filtering of matches - RANSAC
- BoW model for constructing global image descriptors

Introduction

Detection and tracking tasks can be formulated in terms of comparing areas in images. If we're able to find special points in the images and build up descriptors for these points, we can just compare the descriptors and arrive at a conclusion about the similarity of the objects in the images. In Computer Vision, these special points are called keypoints, but several questions arise around this concept: how do you find truly special locations in the images? How do you compute the robust and unique descriptors? And how do you compare these descriptors rapidly and accurately? This chapter addresses all these queries and leads you through all the steps from finding the keypoints to comparing them using OpenCV.

Finding corners in an image - Harris and FAST

A corner can be thought as an intersection of two edges. The mathematical definition of the corners in an image is different, but reflects the same idea; the corner is a point with the following property: moving this point in any direction leads to changes in the small neighborhood of the point. For example, if we take a point on the homogeneous area of an image, moving such a point doesn't change anything in the local window nearby. A point on the edge doesn't belong to a plain region, and once again has directions, movements which don't influence a point's local area: these are movements along the edge. Only corners are movement-sensitive for all directions, and as a consequence, they are good candidates for objects to track or compare. In this recipe, we'll learn how to find corners on an image using two methods from OpenCV.

Getting ready

Before you proceed with this recipe, you need to install the OpenCV version 3.0 (or greater) Python API package.

How to do it...

You need to complete the following steps:

1. Import the necessary modules:

```
import cv2
import numpy as np
```

2. Load an image and find its corners with `cv2.cornerHarris`:

```
img = cv2.imread('../data/scenetext01.jpg', cv2.IMREAD_COLOR)
corners = cv2.cornerHarris(cv2.cvtColor(img, cv2.COLOR_BGR2GRAY),
2, 3, 0.04)
```

3. Process and display the result:

```
corners = cv2.dilate(corners, None)

show_img = np.copy(img)
show_img[corners>0.01*corners.max()]=[0,0,255]
```

```
corners = cv2.normalize(corners, None, 0, 255,
cv2.NORM_MINMAX).astype(np.uint8)
show_img = np.hstack((show_img, cv2.cvtColor(corners,
cv2.COLOR_GRAY2BGR)))

cv2.imshow('Harris corner detector', show_img)
if cv2.waitKey(0) == 27:
    cv2.destroyAllWindows()
```

4. Create a `FAST` detector and apply it to the image:

```
fast = cv2.FastFeatureDetector_create(30, True,
cv2.FAST_FEATURE_DETECTOR_TYPE_9_16)
kp = fast.detect(img)
```

5. Draw the results and show the image:

```
show_img = np.copy(img)
for p in cv2.KeyPoint.convert(kp):
    cv2.circle(show_img, tuple(p), 2, (0, 255, 0), cv2.FILLED)

cv2.imshow('FAST corner detector', show_img)
if cv2.waitKey(0) == 27:
    cv2.destroyAllWindows()
```

6. Disable the non-maximum suppression, retrieve the corners, and display the results:

```
fast.setNonmaxSuppression(False)
kp = fast.detect(img)

for p in cv2.KeyPoint.convert(kp):
    cv2.circle(show_img, tuple(p), 2, (0, 255, 0), cv2.FILLED)
cv2.imshow('FAST corner detector', show_img)
if cv2.waitKey(0) == 27:
    cv2.destroyAllWindows()
```

How it works...

`cv2.cornerHarris` is OpenCV's function which implements, as follows from the name, the `Harris` corners detector. It takes six arguments: the first four arguments are mandatory and last two arguments have default values. The arguments are as follows:

- Single-channel 8-bit or floating-point image, on which corners are to be detected
- Size of the neighborhood window: it should be set to a small value larger than 1

- Size of the window to compute derivatives: it should be set to an odd number
- Sensitivity coefficient for the corners detector: it's usually set to 0.04
- An object where you can store the results
- The borders extrapolation method

The borders extrapolation method determines the manner of image extending. It can be set to a bunch of values (cv2.BORDER_CONSTANT, cv2.BORDER_REPLICATE, and so on), and by default, cv2.BORDER_REFLECT_101 is used. The result of the cv2.cornerHarris call is a map of the Harris measure. Points with higher values are more likely to be good corners. As a result of launching the code related to the Harris corner detector, you will get an image similar to the following (the left part of the image is corners visualization, and the right part is the Harris measure map):

Another method we've applied in this recipe is the **Features from Accelerated Segment Test (FAST)** detector. It also finds corners on an image, but in another way. It considers a circle around each point and computes some statistics on that circle. Let's find out how to use FAST.

First, we need to create a detector using cv2.FastFeatureDetector_create. This function accepts an integer threshold, a flag to enable non-maximum suppression, and a mode that determines both the size of the neighbor area and the number of points threshold. All of these parameters can be modified later using corresponding methods of the cv2.FastFeatureDetector class (setNonmaxSuppression, in the previous code).

To use the detector after the initialization, we need to call the
`cv2.FastFeatureDetector.detect` function. It takes a single-channel image and returns
a list of `cv2.KeyPoint` objects. This list can be converted to a numpy array
by `cv2.KeyPoint.convert`. Each element in the resulting array is a point of the corner.

Execution of the code related to the FAST detector brings up the following images (the left
image for non-maximum suppression enabled, the right image for non-maximum
suppression being disabled):

Selecting good corners in an image for tracking

In this recipe, you will learn how to detect keypoints in an image and apply simple post-
processing heuristics for improving the overall quality of detected keypoints such as getting
rid of keypoint clusters and removing relatively weak keypoints. This functionality is useful
in such computer vision tasks as object tracking and video stabilization, since improving the
quality of detected keypoints affects the final quality of the corresponding algorithms.

Getting ready

Before you proceed with this recipe, you need to install the OpenCV version 3.0 (or greater)
Python API package.

How to do it...

You need to complete the following steps:

1. Import the necessary modules:

```
import cv2
import matplotlib.pyplot as plt
```

2. Load the test image:

```
img = cv2.imread('../data/Lena.png', cv2.IMREAD_GRAYSCALE)
```

3. Find *good* keypoints:

```
corners = cv2.goodFeaturesToTrack(img, 100, 0.05, 10)
```

4. Visualize the results:

```
for c in corners:
    x, y = c[0]
    cv2.circle(img, (x, y), 5, 255, -1)
plt.figure(figsize=(10, 10))
plt.imshow(img, cmap='gray')
plt.tight_layout()
plt.show()
```

How it works...

In this sample, we used the OpenCV function `cv2.goodFeaturesToTrack`. This function detects keypoints and implements a list of heurisitics intended to improve the overall quality of keypoints for such computer vision tasks as object tracking through selecting a subset of *good* keypoints. This function ensures that the keypoints are not located too close to each other, the minimal distance is regulated with the `minDistance` parameter. The `qualityLevel` parameter regulates which keypoints are considered weak with respect to the strongest keypoint, and are removed from the originally detected ones. The function also has the parameter `maxCorners`, which is the maximal number of detected keypoints.

The following output is expected:

Drawing keypoints, descriptors, and matches

After you've found the keypoints, you undoubtedly want to see where these keypoints are in the original image. OpenCV serves as a convenient way to display the keypoints and other related information. Moreover, you can easily draw a correspondence between keypoints from different images. This recipe tells you about how you can visualize keypoints as well as matching results.

Getting ready

Before you proceed with this recipe, you need to install the OpenCV version 3.3 (or greater) Python API package.

How to do it...

You need to complete the following steps:

1. Import the necessary modules:

```
import cv2
import numpy as np
import random
```

2. Load an image, find the FAST keypoints in it, and fill in the size and orientation of each keypoint with random values:

```
img = cv2.imread('../data/scenetext01.jpg', cv2.IMREAD_COLOR)

fast = cv2.FastFeatureDetector_create(160, True,
cv2.FAST_FEATURE_DETECTOR_TYPE_9_16)
keyPoints = fast.detect(img)

for kp in keyPoints:
    kp.size = 100*random.random()
    kp.angle = 360*random.random()

matches = []
for i in range(len(keyPoints)):
    matches.append(cv2.DMatch(i, i, 1))
```

3. Draw the keypoints:

```
show_img = cv2.drawKeypoints(img, keyPoints, None, (255, 0, 255))

cv2.imshow('Keypoints', show_img)
cv2.waitKey()
cv2.destroyAllWindows()
```

4. Visualize the size and orientation information about the keypoints:

```
show_img = cv2.drawKeypoints(img, keyPoints, None, (0, 255, 0),
cv2.DRAW_MATCHES_FLAGS_DRAW_RICH_KEYPOINTS)

cv2.imshow('Keypoints', show_img)
cv2.waitKey()
cv2.destroyAllWindows()
```

5. Show the keypoint's matching results:

```
show_img = cv2.drawMatches(img, keyPoints, img, keyPoints, matches,
None,
flags=cv2.DRAW_MATCHES_FLAGS_DRAW_RICH_KEYPOINTS)

cv2.imshow('Matches', show_img)
cv2.waitKey()
cv2.destroyAllWindows()
```

How it works...

To visualize keypoints, you need to use `cv2.drawKeypoints`. This function takes a source image, a list of keypoints, a destination image, a color, and flags as arguments. In the simplest case, you only need to pass the first three. The source image is used as a background, but it isn't changed by this function, and the result will be placed in the destination image. The list of keypoints is an object, which is returned by the keypoints detector, so you can pass this list directly to the `cv2.drawKeypoints` function without any processing. The color is simply the drawing color. The last parameter, flags, allows you to control the drawing mode—by default, it has the `cv2.DRAW_MATCHES_FLAGS_DEFAULT` value, and in this case, the keypoints are displayed as plain circles of the same diameter. The second option for this flag is `cv2.DRAW_MATCHES_FLAGS_DRAW_RICH_KEYPOINTS`. In this case, the points will be drawn as circles with different diameters, and the orientation will also be displayed with a line from the center of the circle. The drawn diameter of the keypoint shows the neighborhood, which was used to compute the keypoint; orientation shows specific direction for the keypoint, if the keypoint has such one. `cv2.drawKeypoints` returns the resulting image with drawn keypoints.

`cv2.drawMatches` helps you show the correspondences you have between points after the keypoints matching process. The arguments of this function are: the first image and the list of keypoints for it, the second image and its keypoints, a list of match results for the keypoints, a destination image, a color for drawing correspondences, a color for drawing keyponts without matches, a mask for drawing matches, and a flag. Usually, you have values for the first five parameters after keypoints detection and matching. Colors for matched and unmatched (single) points are generated randomly by default, but you can set them with any values. A mask for matches is a list of values where a non-zero value means the corresponding match (with the same index) should be displayed. By default, the mask is empty and all matches are drawn. The last argument controls the mode of keypoints being displayed. It can be set to `cv2.DRAW_MATCHES_FLAGS_DEFAULT` or `cv2.DRAW_MATCHES_FLAGS_DRAW_RICH_KEYPOINTS` and optionally conjugated with the `cv2.DRAW_MATCHES_FLAGS_NOT_DRAW_SINGLE_POINTS` value.

The first two values have the same meaning as the `cv2.drawKeypoints` function. The final value, `cv2.DRAW_MATCHES_FLAGS_NOT_DRAW_SINGLE_POINTS`, allows you to not show the keypoints without matches.

You will get an image similar to the following as a result of the code execution:

Detecting scale invariant keypoints

Objects in the real world are moving, making it harder to accurately compare them with their previous appearances. When they approach the camera, the objects get bigger. To deal with this situation, we should be able to detect keypoints that are insensitive to an object's size differences. **Scale Invariant Feature Transform** (**SIFT**) descriptors have been designed especially to handle different object scales and find the same features for the objects, no matter what their size is. This recipe shows you how to use SIFT implementation from OpenCV.

Getting ready

Before you proceed with this recipe, you need to install the OpenCV version 3.0 (or greater) Python API package with contrib modules.

How to do it...

You need to complete the following steps:

1. Import the necessary modules and load images:

```
import cv2
import numpy as np

img0 = cv2.imread('../data/Lena.png', cv2.IMREAD_COLOR)
img1 = cv2.imread('../data/Lena_rotated.png', cv2.IMREAD_COLOR)
img1 = cv2.resize(img1, None, fx=0.75, fy=0.75)
img1 = np.pad(img1, ((64,)*2, (64,)*2, (0,)*2), 'constant',
constant_values=0)
imgs_list = [img0, img1]
```

2. Create a SIFT keypoints detector:

```
detector = cv2.xfeatures2d.SIFT_create(50)
```

3. Detect the keypoints in each image, visualize the keypoints and display the result:

```
for i in range(len(imgs_list)):
    keypoints, descriptors =
detector.detectAndCompute(imgs_list[i], None)
    imgs_list[i] = cv2.drawKeypoints(imgs_list[i], keypoints, None,
```

```
                (0, 255, 0),
                flags=cv2.DRAW_MATCHES_FLAGS_DRAW_RICH_KEYPOINTS)
    cv2.imshow('SIFT keypoints', np.hstack(imgs_list))
    cv2.waitKey()
    cv2.destroyAllWindows()
```

How it works...

To create an instance of the SIFT keypoints detector, you need to use the cv2.xfeatures2d.SIFT_create function. All its arguments have default values, and the arguments themselves are: the number of keypoints to find and return, the number of levels in the scale pyramid to use, the two thresholds to tune the sensitivity of the algorithm, and the sigma variance for presmoothing the image. All of the arguments are important, but the ones you probably need to tunr in the first place are the number of keypoints and the sigma. The last one controls the maximal size of the objects you don't care about and can be useful to remove the noise and extra small details from the image.

As a result of completing the code from the recipe, you will get an image similar to the following:

As you can see, the same configurations of the keypoints are found in the images despite the fact that the right image is tilted a bit and has smaller size than the right one. This is the key feature of SIFT descriptors.

Computing descriptors for image keypoints - SURF, BRIEF, ORB

In the previous recipes, we've examined several ways of finding keypoints in the image. Basically, keypoints are just locations of extraordinary areas. But how do we distinguish between these locations? This question arises in many situations, especially in video processing, when we want to track an object in a sequence of frames. This recipe covers some effective approaches of characterizing keypoint neighborhoods, in other words, computing keypoint descriptors.

Getting ready

Before you proceed with this recipe, you need to install the OpenCV version 3.0 (or greater) Python API package with contrib modules.

How to do it...

You need to complete the steps:

1. Import the modules we need and load an image:

```
import cv2
import numpy as np

img = cv2.imread('../data/scenetext01.jpg', cv2.IMREAD_COLOR)
```

2. Create a SURF feature detector and tune some of its parameters. Then, apply it to the loaded image and display the result:

```
surf = cv2.xfeatures2d.SURF_create(10000)
surf.setExtended(True)
surf.setNOctaves(3)
surf.setNOctaveLayers(10)
surf.setUpright(False)

keyPoints, descriptors = surf.detectAndCompute(img, None)

show_img = cv2.drawKeypoints(img, keyPoints, None, (255, 0, 0),
cv2.DRAW_MATCHES_FLAGS_DRAW_RICH_KEYPOINTS)

cv2.imshow('SURF descriptors', show_img)
```

```
cv2.waitKey()
cv2.destroyAllWindows()
```

3. Create a BRIEF keypoint descriptor and apply it to the SURF keypoints. After this, display the resulting keypoints:

```
brief = cv2.xfeatures2d.BriefDescriptorExtractor_create(32, True)

keyPoints, descriptors = brief.compute(img, keyPoints)

show_img = cv2.drawKeypoints(img, keyPoints, None, (0, 255, 0),
cv2.DRAW_MATCHES_FLAGS_DRAW_RICH_KEYPOINTS)

cv2.imshow('BRIEF descriptors', show_img)
cv2.waitKey()
cv2.destroyAllWindows()
```

4. Initialize an ORB features detector. After this, detect the keypoints and compute the descriptors for the image. Then, draw the keypoints in the image:

```
orb = cv2.ORB_create()

orb.setMaxFeatures(200)

keyPoints = orb.detect(img, None)
keyPoints, descriptors = orb.compute(img, keyPoints)

show_img = cv2.drawKeypoints(img, keyPoints, None, (0, 0, 255),
cv2.DRAW_MATCHES_FLAGS_DRAW_RICH_KEYPOINTS)

cv2.imshow('ORB descriptors', show_img)
cv2.waitKey()
cv2.destroyAllWindows()
```

How it works...

All of the previously used keypoint descriptors implement the cv2.Feature2D interface and have the same fashion of use. All of them require the creation of the descriptor object as a first step. Then, there is a possibility to set or tune some parameters of the created descriptor. It's worth mentioning that the descriptors have default values for the parameters of algorithms, and these chosen default values work well in many cases. When the descriptor is ready to be used, the detect, compute, and detectAndCompute methods should be used to retrieve keypoints and/or descriptors for the specified image.

To create SURF descriptors, you need to call the
`cv2.xfeatures2d.SURF_create` function. It takes a considerable number of arguments, but fortunately all of them have default values. This function returns the initialized SURF descriptor object. To apply it to the image, you can find both keypoints and their descriptors by invoking the `detectAndCompute` function. You need to pass an input image to this function, an input image mask (can be set to None if there is no mask provided), an object to store the computed descriptors, and a flag for whether you should use precomputed keypoints or not. The function returns a list of keypoints and a list of descriptors for each returned keypoint.

To create a BRIEF descriptor, you need to use the
`cv2.BriefDescriptorExtractor_create` function. This function takes the algorithm's parameters as arguments and returns an initialized descriptor object. The BRIEF descriptor can't detect keypoints and therefore implements only the `compute` method, which returns descriptors for input images and previously detected keypoints.

The ORB keypoints detector can be created with the `cv2.ORB_create` function. Again, this function takes a bunch of specifics to this algorithm's arguments and returns a constructed and ready-to-use object.

The code from the recipe results in the following image:

Matching techniques for finding correspondences between descriptors

We want to find a correspondence between keypoints in detection and tracking tasks, but we can't compare the points themselves; instead, we should deal with keypoints descriptors. Keypoints descriptors were especially developed to make it possible to compare them. This recipe shows you OpenCV's approaches to comparing the descriptors and building up the correspondence between them using various matching techniques.

Getting ready

Before you proceed with this recipe, you need to install the OpenCV version 3.3 (or greater) Python API package.

How to do it...

You need to complete the following steps:

1. Import the necessary modules:

```
import cv2
import numpy as np
```

2. Define a function which handles a video file. This function takes each frame, match the keypoints for this frame and the one 40 frames before:

```
def video_keypoints(matcher,
cap=cv2.VideoCapture("../data/traffic.mp4"),
                detector=cv2.ORB_create(40)):
    cap.set(cv2.CAP_PROP_POS_FRAMES, 0)
    while True:
        status_cap, frame = cap.read()
        frame = cv2.resize(frame, (0, 0), fx=0.5, fy=0.5)
        if not status_cap:
            break
        if (cap.get(cv2.CAP_PROP_POS_FRAMES) - 1) % 40 == 0:
            key_frame = np.copy(frame)
            key_points_1, descriptors_1 =
detector.detectAndCompute(frame, None)
        else:
            key_points_2, descriptors_2 =
```

```
detector.detectAndCompute(frame, None)
            matches = matcher.match(descriptors_2, descriptors_1)
            frame = cv2.drawMatches(frame, key_points_2, key_frame,
key_points_1,
                                    matches, None,
flags=cv2.DRAW_MATCHES_FLAGS_DRAW_RICH_KEYPOINTS |
cv2.DRAW_MATCHES_FLAGS_NOT_DRAW_SINGLE_POINTS)
        cv2.imshow('Keypoints matching', frame)
        if cv2.waitKey(300) == 27:
            break

    cv2.destroyAllWindows()
```

3. Compare the frames with brute-force matching:

```
bf_matcher = cv2.BFMatcher_create(cv2.NORM_HAMMING2, True)
video_keypoints(bf_matcher)
```

4. Apply KD-tree indexing to the SURF descriptors:

```
flann_kd_matcher = cv2.FlannBasedMatcher()
video_keypoints(flann_kd_matcher,
detector=cv2.xfeatures2d.SURF_create(20000))
```

5. Use **Local-Sensitive Hash (LSH)** for binary ORB features:

```
FLANN_INDEX_LSH = 6
index_params = dict(algorithm=FLANN_INDEX_LSH, table_number=20,
key_size=15, multi_probe_level=2)
search_params = dict(checks=10)

flann_kd_matcher = cv2.FlannBasedMatcher(index_params,
search_params)
video_keypoints(flann_kd_matcher)
```

6. Rerun the process with the composite KD-tree plus k-means indexing algorithm:

```
FLANN_INDEX_COMPOSITE = 3
index_params = dict(algorithm=FLANN_INDEX_COMPOSITE, trees=16)
search_params = dict(checks=10)

flann_kd_matcher = cv2.FlannBasedMatcher(index_params,
search_params)
video_keypoints(flann_kd_matcher,
detector=cv2.xfeatures2d.SURF_create(20000))
```

How it works...

OpenCV supports a lot of different matching types. All of them are implemented using the `cv2.DescriptorMatcher` interface, so any type of matcher supports the same methods and the same scenarios of use. There are two types of matcher usage: detecting mode and tracking mode. Technically, there is not a big difference between these two modes because in both cases, we need to have two sets of descriptors to match them. The question is whether we upload the first set once and compare it with another one, or each time pass two descriptor sets to the match function. To upload the descriptor set, you need to use the `cv2.DescriptorMatcher.add` function, which just accepts a list of your descriptors. After you've finished adding the descriptors, in some cases, you need to call the `cv2.DescriptorMatcher.train` method to tell the matcher handle about the descriptors and prepare them for the matching process.

`cv2.DescriptorMatcher` has several methods to perform matching, and all of these methods have overloads for detecting and tracking modes. `cv2.DescriptorMatcher.match` is used to get the single best correspondence between descriptors. `cv2.DescriptorMatcher.knnMatch` and `cv2.DescriptorMatcher.radiusMatch` return several of the best correspondences between descriptors.

The simplest and most obvious approach to find the best descriptor matches is to just compare all possible pairs and choose the best. Needless to say, this method is extremely slow. But if you decide to use it (for example, as a reference), you need to call the `cv2.BFMatcher_create` function. It takes a type of distance metric for descriptor comparison and enables the cross-checking flag.

To create smarter and faster matchers, you need to call `cv2.FlannBasedMatcher`. By default, it creates KD-tree indexing with default parameters. To create other types of matchers and set up their parameters, you need to pass two dictionaries for the `cv2.FlannBasedMatcher` function. First, the dictionary describes the algorithm for indexing descriptors and its parameters. The second argument describes the process of searching for the best match.

After you launch the code, you will get an image similar to the following:

Finding reliable matches - cross-check and ratio test

In this recipe, you will learn how filter keypoint matches using cross-check and ratio tests. These techniques are useful for filtering bad matches and improving the overall quality of established correspondences.

Getting ready

Before you proceed with this recipe, you need to install the OpenCV version 3.3 (or greater) Python API package.

How to do it...

You need to complete the following steps:

1. Import the necessary modules:

   ```
   import cv2
   import matplotlib.pyplot as plt
   ```

2. Load the test images:

   ```
   img0 = cv2.imread('../data/Lena.png', cv2.IMREAD_GRAYSCALE)
   img1 = cv2.imread('../data/Lena_rotated.png', cv2.IMREAD_GRAYSCALE)
   ```

3. Create the detector, detect keypoints, and computer descriptors:

```
detector = cv2.ORB_create(100)
kps0, fea0 = detector.detectAndCompute(img0, None)
kps1, fea1 = detector.detectAndCompute(img1, None)
```

4. Create the *k*-nearest neighbor descriptor matcher with *k*=2, and find matches from left to right and vice versa:

```
matcher = cv2.BFMatcher_create(cv2.NORM_HAMMING, False)
matches01 = matcher.knnMatch(fea0, fea1, k=2)
matches10 = matcher.knnMatch(fea1, fea0, k=2)
```

5. Create a function for filter matching using the ratio test, and filter all the matches:

```
def ratio_test(matches, ratio_thr):
    good_matches = []
    for m in matches:
        ratio = m[0].distance / m[1].distance
        if ratio < ratio_thr:
            good_matches.append(m[0])
    return good_matches

RATIO_THR = 0.7 # Lower values mean more aggressive filtering.
good_matches01 = ratio_test(matches01, RATIO_THR)
good_matches10 = ratio_test(matches10, RATIO_THR)
```

6. Do the cross-check matches test—only leave the ones that are present in both left-to-right and right-to-left lists:

```
good_matches10_ = {(m.trainIdx, m.queryIdx) for m in
good_matches10}
final_matches = [m for m in good_matches01 if (m.queryIdx,
m.trainIdx)
                 in good_matches10_]
```

7. Visualize the results:

```
dbg_img = cv2.drawMatches(img0, kps0, img1, kps1, final_matches,
None)
plt.figure()
plt.imshow(dbg_img[:,:,[2,1,0]])
plt.tight_layout()
plt.show()
```

How it works...

In this recipe, we implement two heuristics for filtering bad matches. The first one is the ratio test. It checks whether the best matche is significantly better than the second best one. The check is performed through comparing matching scores. Two best matches for each keypoint are found using the `knnMatch` method of the `cv2.BFMatcher` class.

The second heuristic is the cross-check test. For two images, *A* and *B*, it checks whether the matches found in *B* for keypoints in *A* are the same as the ones found in *A* for keypoints in *B*. The correspondences that were found in both directions are retained, and the other ones are removed.

The following is the expected output:

Model-based filtering of matches - RANSAC

In this recipe, you will learn how to robustly filter matches between keypoints in two images using the **Random Sample Consensus** (**RANSAC**) algorithm under the assumption that there's a homography transformation between the two images. This technique helps filter out bad matches and only leaves the ones that satisfy the motion model between two images.

Getting ready

Before you proceed with this recipe, you need to install the OpenCV version 3.3 (or greater) Python API package.

How to do it...

You need to complete the following steps:

1. Import the necessary modules:

```
import cv2
import numpy as np
import matplotlib.pyplot as plt
```

2. Load the test images:

```
img0 = cv2.imread('../data/Lena.png', cv2.IMREAD_GRAYSCALE)
img1 = cv2.imread('../data/Lena_rotated.png', cv2.IMREAD_GRAYSCALE)
```

3. Detect the keypoints and computer descriptors:

```
detector = cv2.ORB_create(100)
kps0, fea0 = detector.detectAndCompute(img0, None)
kps1, fea1 = detector.detectAndCompute(img1, None)
matcher = cv2.BFMatcher_create(cv2.NORM_HAMMING, False)
matches = matcher.match(fea0, fea1)
```

4. Fit the homography model into the found keypoint correspondences robustly and get a mask of inlier matches:

```
pts0 = np.float32([kps0[m.queryIdx].pt for m in
matches]).reshape(-1,2)
pts1 = np.float32([kps1[m.trainIdx].pt for m in
matches]).reshape(-1,2)
H, mask = cv2.findHomography(pts0, pts1, cv2.RANSAC, 3.0)
```

5. Visualize the results:

```
plt.figure()
plt.subplot(211)
plt.axis('off')
plt.title('all matches')
dbg_img = cv2.drawMatches(img0, kps0, img1, kps1, matches, None)
plt.imshow(dbg_img[:,:,[2,1,0]])
```

```
plt.subplot(212)
plt.axis('off')
plt.title('filtered matches')
dbg_img = cv2.drawMatches(img0, kps0, img1, kps1, [m for i,m in
enumerate(matches) if mask[i]], None)
plt.imshow(dbg_img[:,:,[2,1,0]])
plt.tight_layout()
plt.show()
```

How it works...

In this recipe, we estimate homography model parameters between two images using the robust RANSAC algorithm. It's done through the `cv2.findHomography` function with the `cv2.RANSAC` parameter. The function returns a homography transformation estimated by point correspondences as well as the inliers mask. The inlier mask deals with correspondences that satisfy the estimated motion model with a low enough error. In our case, the error is computed as a Euclidean distance between the matched point and the corresponding point transformed according to the motion model.

The following is the expected output:

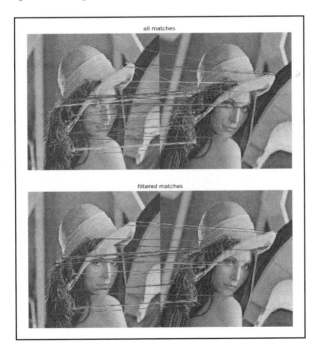

BoW model for constructing global image descriptors

In this recipe, you will learn how to apply the **Bag-of-Words** (**BoW**) model for computing global image descriptors. This technique can be used for building a machine learning model to solve image classification problems.

Getting ready

Before you proceed with this recipe, you need to install the OpenCV version 3.3 (or greater) Python API package.

How to do it...

You need to complete the following steps:

1. Import the necessary modules:

```
import cv2
import numpy as np
import matplotlib.pyplot as plt
```

2. Load the two train images:

```
img0 = cv2.imread('../data/people.jpg', cv2.IMREAD_GRAYSCALE)
img1 = cv2.imread('../data/face.jpeg', cv2.IMREAD_GRAYSCALE)
```

3. Detect the keypoints and computer descriptors for each training image:

```
detector = cv2.ORB_create(500)
_, fea0 = detector.detectAndCompute(img0, None)
_, fea1 = detector.detectAndCompute(img1, None)
descr_type = fea0.dtype
```

4. Construct the BoW vocabulary:

```
bow_trainer = cv2.BOWKMeansTrainer(50)
bow_trainer.add(np.float32(fea0))
bow_trainer.add(np.float32(fea1))
vocab = bow_trainer.cluster().astype(descr_type))
```

5. Create an object for computing global image BoW descriptors:

```
bow_descr = cv2.BOWImgDescriptorExtractor(detector,
cv2.BFMatcher(cv2.NORM_HAMMING))
bow_descr.setVocabulary(vocab)
```

6. Load the test image, find the keypoints, and the compute global image descriptor:

```
img = cv2.imread('../data/Lena.png', cv2.IMREAD_GRAYSCALE)
kps = detector.detect(img, None)
descr = bow_descr.compute(img, kps)
```

7. Visualize the descriptor:

```
plt.figure(figsize=(10,8))
plt.title('image BoW descriptor')
plt.bar(np.arange(len(descr[0])), descr[0])
plt.xlabel('vocabulary element')
plt.ylabel('frequency')
plt.tight_layout()
plt.show()
```

How it works...

The Bag-of-Words model works in two phases. In the training phase, one collects local image descriptors for training images (img0 and img1, in our case) and clusters them into vocabulary. In the second phase, local descriptors found in the input image are compared with all vocabulary *words*, alongside a list of how often each *word* appeared (for example, was selected as the closest one) within the image, for example, the frequencies vector, which forms the global image descriptor.

The following is the expected output:

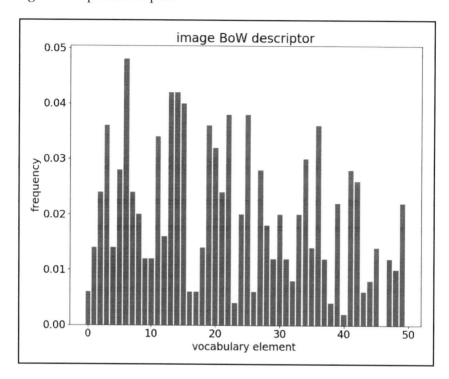

8

Image and Video Processing

This chapter contains recipes for:

- Warping an image using affine and perspective transformations
- Remapping an image using arbitrary transformation
- Tracking keypoints between frames using the Lucas-Kanade algorithm
- Background subtraction
- Stitching many images into panorama
- Denoising a photo using non-local means algorithms
- Constructing an HDR image
- Removing defects from a photo with image inpainting

Introduction

By working with a group of images as a whole set instead of as a bunch of separate and independent images, Computer Vision algorithms can achieve way more fabulous results. If correlations between images are known (it may be a sequence of frames in a video file of some object shot from different perspectives), we can exploit them. This chapter uses algorithms that take into account relations between frames. The algorithms are background subtraction, images stitching, video stabilization, superrelosution, and constructing HDR images.

Warping an image using affine and perspective transformations

In this recipe, we will review two main ways to geometrically transform images: affine and perspective warps. The first one is used to remove simple geometrical transformations such as rotations, scales, translations, and their combinations, but it can't turn converging lines into parallel ones. Here, perspective transformation comes into play. It aims to eliminate perspective distortions when two parallel lines converge in perspective views. Let's find out how to use all these transformations in OpenCV.

Getting ready

Before you proceed with this recipe, you need to install the OpenCV version 3.3 (or greater) Python API package.

How to do it

You need to complete the following steps:

1. Import the necessary modules, open an input image, and copy it:

    ```python
    import cv2
    import numpy as np

    img = cv2.imread('../data/circlesgrid.png', cv2.IMREAD_COLOR)
    show_img = np.copy(img)
    ```

2. Define two functions to implement the process of points selection :

    ```python
    selected_pts = []

    def mouse_callback(event, x, y, flags, param):
        global selected_pts, show_img

        if event == cv2.EVENT_LBUTTONUP:
            selected_pts.append([x, y])
            cv2.circle(show_img, (x, y), 10, (0, 255, 0), 3)

    def select_points(image, points_num):
        global selected_pts
        selected_pts = []
    ```

```
cv2.namedWindow('image')
cv2.setMouseCallback('image', mouse_callback)

while True:
    cv2.imshow('image', image)

    k = cv2.waitKey(1)

    if k == 27 or len(selected_pts) == points_num:
        break

cv2.destroyAllWindows()

return np.array(selected_pts, dtype=np.float32)
```

3. Select three points in the image, compute the affine transformation with `cv2.getAffineTransform`, and apply it with `cv2.warpAffine`. Then, show the resulting images:

```
show_img = np.copy(img)
src_pts = select_points(show_img, 3)
dst_pts = np.array([[0, 240], [0, 0], [240, 0]], dtype=np.float32)

affine_m = cv2.getAffineTransform(src_pts, dst_pts)

unwarped_img = cv2.warpAffine(img, affine_m, (240, 240))

cv2.imshow('result', np.hstack((show_img, unwarped_img)))
k = cv2.waitKey()

cv2.destroyAllWindows()
```

4. Find an inverse affine transformation, apply it, and display the results:

```
inv_affine = cv2.invertAffineTransform(affine_m)
warped_img = cv2.warpAffine(unwarped_img, inv_affine, (320, 240))

cv2.imshow('result', np.hstack((show_img, unwarped_img,
warped_img)))
k = cv2.waitKey()

cv2.destroyAllWindows()
```

5. Create a rotation-scale affine warp with `cv2.getRotationMatrix2D` and apply it to the image:

```
rotation_mat = cv2.getRotationMatrix2D(tuple(src_pts[0]), 6, 1)

rotated_img = cv2.warpAffine(img, rotation_mat, (240, 240))

cv2.imshow('result', np.hstack((show_img, rotated_img)))
k = cv2.waitKey()

cv2.destroyAllWindows()
```

6. Select four points in the image, create a matrix for perspective warp with `cv2.getPerspectiveTransform`, and then apply it to the image and display the results:

```
show_img = np.copy(img)
src_pts = select_points(show_img, 4)
dst_pts = np.array([[0, 240], [0, 0], [240, 0], [240, 240]],
dtype=np.float32)

perspective_m = cv2.getPerspectiveTransform(src_pts, dst_pts)

unwarped_img = cv2.warpPerspective(img, perspective_m, (240, 240))

cv2.imshow('result', np.hstack((show_img, unwarped_img)))
k = cv2.waitKey()

cv2.destroyAllWindows()
```

How it works

Both affine and perspective transformations are essentially matrix multiplication operations, where positions of elements are remapped with some warp matrix. So, to apply a transformation we need to compute such a warp matrix. For affine transformation, this can be done with the `cv2.getAffineTransform` function. It takes two set of points as arguments: the first one contains three points before transformation, and the second one contains three corresponding points after warp. The order of points in the sets does matter, and it should be the same for both arrays. To create the transformation matrix in the case of perspective warp, `cv2.getPerspectiveTransform` can be applied.

Again, it accepts two sets of points before and after warp, but the length of points sets should be 4. Both functions return the transformation matrix, but they are different shapes: `cv2.getAffineTransform` computes a 2x3 matrix and `cv2.getPerspectiveTransform` computes a 3x3 matrix.

To apply the computed transformations, we need to invoke the corresponding OpenCV functions. To perform affine warp, `cv2.warpAffine` is used. It takes a input image, a 2x3 transformation matrix, an output image size, pixels interpolation mode, border extrapolation mode, and a border extrapolation value. `cv2.warpPerspective` is used to apply perspective transformation. Its arguments have the same meaning as `cv2.warpAffine`. The only difference is that the transformation matrix (second argument) must be 3x3. Both functions return a warped image.

There are two useful functions related to affine transformation: `cv2.invertAffineTransform` and `cv2.getRotationMatrix2D`. The first is used when you have some affine transformation and need to get an inverse one (also affine). It takes this existing affine transformation and returns the inverted one. `cv2.getRotationMatrix2D` is less general but is often used in the case of affine transformation - rotation with scale. This function takes the following arguments: the center point of rotation in (x, y) format, the angle of rotation, and the scale factor, and returns a 2x3 affine transformation matrix. This matrix can be used as a corresponding argument in `cv2.warpAffine`.

After launching the code you will get images similar to the following:

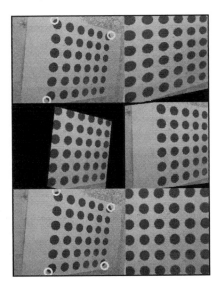

The first row in the figure is an input image with three selected points and its corresponding affine transformation; the second row is the result of an inverse transformation and a rotation with scale transformation; the third row contains the input image with four selected points and is the result of perspective transformation.

Remapping an image using arbitrary transformation

In this recipe, you will learn how to transform images using per-pixel mappings. This is a piece of functionality that is very generic and is used in many computer vision applications, such as image stitching, camera frames undistortion, and many others.

Getting ready

Before you proceed with this recipe, you need to install the OpenCV version 3.3 (or greater) Python API package.

How to do it

You need to complete the following steps:

1. Import the necessary modules:

```
import math
import cv2
import numpy as np
```

2. Load the test images:

```
img = cv2.imread('../data/Lena.png')
```

3. Prepare the per-pixel transformation maps:

```
xmap = np.zeros((img.shape[1], img.shape[0]), np.float32)
ymap = np.zeros((img.shape[1], img.shape[0]), np.float32)
for y in range(img.shape[0]):
    for x in range(img.shape[1]):
        xmap[y,x] = x + 30 * math.cos(20 * x / img.shape[0])
        ymap[y,x] = y + 30 * math.sin(20 * y / img.shape[1])
```

4. Remap the source image:

```
remapped_img = cv2.remap(img, xmap, ymap, cv2.INTER_LINEAR, None,
cv2.BORDER_REPLICATE)
```

5. Visualize the results:

```
plt.figure(0)
plt.axis('off')
plt.imshow(remapped_img[:,:,[2,1,0]])
plt.show()
```

How it works

Generic per-pixel transformation is implemented by the cv2.remap function. It accepts a source image and two maps (which can be passed as one map with two channels), and returns a transformed image. The function also accepts parameters specifying how pixel value interpolation and extrapolation must be performed. In our case, we specify bilinear interpolation, and out-of-range values are replaced with the closest (spatially) in-range pixel values. The function is very generic and often used as a building block of many computer vision applications.

The following is the expected outcome:

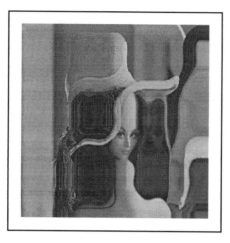

Tracking keypoints between frames using the Lucas-Kanade algorithm

In this recipe, you will learn how to track keypoints between frames in videos using the sparse Lucas-Kanade optical flow algorithm. This functionality is useful in many computer vision applications, such as object tracking and video stabilization.

Getting ready

Before you proceed with this recipe, you need to install the OpenCV version 3.3 (or greater) Python API package.

How to do it

You need to complete the following steps:

1. Import the necessary modules:

```
import cv2
```

2. Open a test video and initialize the auxiliary variables:

```
video = cv2.VideoCapture('../data/traffic.mp4')
prev_pts = None
prev_gray_frame = None
tracks = None
```

3. Start reading the frames from the video, converting each image into grayscale:

```
while True:
    retval, frame = video.read()
    if not retval: break
    gray_frame = cv2.cvtColor(frame, cv2.COLOR_BGR2GRAY)
```

4. Track the keypoints from a previous frame using the sparse Lucas-Kanade optical flow algorithm or, if you've just started or pressed *C*, detect the keypoints so that we have something to track in the next frame:

```
if prev_pts is not None:
    pts, status, errors = cv2.calcOpticalFlowPyrLK(
        prev_gray_frame, gray_frame, prev_pts, None,
winSize=(15,15), maxLevel=5,
        criteria=(cv2.TERM_CRITERIA_EPS |
cv2.TERM_CRITERIA_COUNT, 10, 0.03))
    good_pts = pts[status == 1]
    if tracks is None: tracks = good_pts
    else: tracks = np.vstack((tracks, good_pts))
    for p in tracks:
        cv2.circle(frame, (p[0], p[1]), 3, (0, 255, 0), -1)
else:
    pts = cv2.goodFeaturesToTrack(gray_frame, 500, 0.05, 10)
    pts = pts.reshape(-1, 1, 2)
```

5. Remember the current points and current frame. Now visualize the results and handle the keyboard input:

```
prev_pts = pts
prev_gray_frame = gray_frame
cv2.imshow('frame', frame)
key = cv2.waitKey() & 0xff
if key == 27: break
if key == ord('c'):
    tracks = None
    prev_pts = None
```

6. Close all windows:

```
cv2.destroyAllWindows()
```

How it works

In this recipe, we open a video, detect the initial keypoints using the `cv2.goodFeaturesToTrack` function that we used earlier, and start tracking points using the sparse Lucas-Kanade optical flow algorithm, which has been implemented in OpenCV with the `cv2.calcOpticalFlowPyrLK` function. OpenCV implements a pyramidal version of the algorithm, meaning that the optical flow is first calculated in an image of a smaller size, and then refined in a bigger image. The pyramid size is controlled with the `maxLevel` parameter. The function also takes parameters of the Lucas-Kanade algorithm, such as window size (`winSize`) and termination criteria. The other parameters are previous and current frames, and keypoints from the previous frame. The functions return tracked points in the current frame, an array of success flags, and tracking errors.

The following image is an example of a points tracking result:

Background subtraction

If you have a video of a steady scene with some objects moving around, it's possible to separate a still background from a changing foreground. Here, we will show you how to do it in OpenCV.

Getting ready

Before you proceed with this recipe, you need to install the OpenCV version 3.3 (or greater) Python API package with contrib modules.

How to do it

You need to complete the following steps:

1. Import the necessary modules:

```
import cv2
import numpy as np
```

2. Define a function that opens a video file and applies a few background subtraction algorithms to each frame:

```
def split_image_fgbg(subtractor, open_sz=(0,0), close_sz=(0,0),
show_bg=False, show_shdw=False):
    kernel_open = kernel_close = None
    if all(i > 0 for i in open_sz):
        kernel_open = cv2.getStructuringElement(cv2.MORPH_ELLIPSE,
open_sz)
    if all(i > 0 for i in close_sz):
        kernel_close = cv2.getStructuringElement(cv2.MORPH_ELLIPSE,
close_sz)

    cap = cv2.VideoCapture('../data/traffic.mp4')
    while True:
        status_cap, frame = cap.read()
        if not status_cap:
            break
        frame = cv2.resize(frame, None, fx=0.5, fy=0.5)
        fgmask = subtractor.apply(frame)
        objects_mask = (fgmask == 255).astype(np.uint8)
        shadows_mask = (fgmask == 127).astype(np.uint8)
        if kernel_open is not None:
            objects_mask = cv2.morphologyEx(objects_mask,
cv2.MORPH_OPEN, kernel_open)

        if kernel_close is not None:
            objects_mask = cv2.morphologyEx(objects_mask,
cv2.MORPH_CLOSE, kernel_close)
            if kernel_open is not None:
                shadows_mask = cv2.morphologyEx(shadows_mask,
```

```
cv2.MORPH_CLOSE, kernel_open)
        foreground = frame
        foreground[objects_mask == 0] = 0
        if show_shdw:
            foreground[shadows_mask > 0] = (0, 255, 0)
        cv2.imshow('foreground', foreground)

        if show_bg:
            background = fgbg.getBackgroundImage()
            if background is not None:
                cv2.imshow('background', background)

        if cv2.waitKey(30) == 27:
            break

    cap.release()
    cv2.destroyAllWindows()
```

3. Apply the Gaussian Mixture-based Background/Foreground Segmentation Algorithm created by KadewTraKuPong and Bowden to the video:

```
fgbg = cv2.bgsegm.createBackgroundSubtractorMOG()

split_image_fgbg(fgbg, (2, 2), (40, 40))
```

4. Create an instance of an improved version of the Gaussian Mixture segmentation algorithm developed by Zoran Zivkovic:

```
fgbg = cv2.createBackgroundSubtractorMOG2()

split_image_fgbg(fgbg, (3, 3), (30, 30), True)
```

5. Use the background subtraction algorithm of Godbehere, Matsukawa, and Goldberg to create background masks:

```
fgbg = cv2.bgsegm.createBackgroundSubtractorGMG()

split_image_fgbg(fgbg, (5, 5), (25, 25))
```

6. Apply the background subtraction algorithm based on counting, as suggested by Sagi Zeevi:

```
fgbg = cv2.bgsegm.createBackgroundSubtractorCNT()

split_image_fgbg(fgbg, (5, 5), (15, 15), True)
```

7. Employ the background segmentation technique based on the Nearest Neighbors method:

```
fgbg = cv2.createBackgroundSubtractorKNN()

split_image_fgbg(fgbg, (5, 5), (25, 25), True)
```

How it works

All background subtractors implement the `cv2.BackgroundSubtractor` interface, therefore all of them have a certain set of methods:

- `cv2.BackgroundSubtractor.apply`: to get the segmentation mask
- `cv2.BackgroundSubtractor.getBackgroundImage`: to retrieve a background image

The `apply` method accepts a colorful image as an argument and returns a background mask. This mask generally consists of three values: 0 for background pixels, 255 for foreground pixels, and 127 for shadow pixels. Shadow pixels are pixels in the background with lower intensity. It's worth mentioning that not all subtractors support analysis of shadow pixels.

`getBackgroundImage` returns a background image as it should be if there are no moving objects. Again, only a few subtractors are able to compute such an image.

Not surprisingly, all of the subtraction algorithms have internal parameters. Fortunately, many of these parameters work well with default values. One of the parameters, which can be tuned first, is history. Basically, it's a number of frames the subtractor needs to analyse before it starts to produce a segmentation mask. So, usually you get full background masks for first frames.

As you've noticed, we apply morphology operations to the moving objects masks. We need this step for to several reasons. First, some parts of the moving objects may have poor textures. This makes it harder to detect motion because all neighbor pixels are very similar. The second reason is our background segmentation detector isn't as accurate as we want. It makes mistakes by wrongly marking parts of moving objects as a background. Applying morphology helps us use prior information which can't be still parts inside moving objects.

The preceding code produces images similar to the following figure:

Stitching many images into panorama

OpenCV has a lot of Computer Vision algorithms. Some of them are low-level, while others are used in special cases. But there is functionality, which joins many algorithms together using everyday applications. One of these pipelines is panorama stitching. This rather complicated procedure can be done easily in OpenCV and gives decent results. This recipe shows you how to use OpenCV tools to create your own panorama.

Getting ready

Before you proceed with this recipe, you need to install the OpenCV version 3.3 (or greater) Python API package.

How to do it

You need to complete the following steps:

1. Import the necessary modules:

   ```
   import cv2
   import numpy as np
   ```

2. Load the images we're going to combine into a panorama:

   ```
   images = []
   images.append(cv2.imread('../data/panorama/0.jpg',
   cv2.IMREAD_COLOR))
   images.append(cv2.imread('../data/panorama/1.jpg',
   cv2.IMREAD_COLOR))
   ```

3. Create a panorama stitcher, pass your images to it, and parse the result:

   ```
   stitcher = cv2.createStitcher()
   ret, pano = stitcher.stitch(images)

   if ret == cv2.STITCHER_OK:
       cv2.imshow('panorama', pano)
       cv2.waitKey()

       cv2.destroyAllWindows()
   else:
       print('Error during stiching')
   ```

How it works

`cv2.createStitcher` builds an instance of the panorama stitching algorithm. To apply it to the panorama creation, you need to call its `stitch` method. This method accepts an array of images to combine, and returns a stitching result status as well as a panorama image. The status may have one of the following values:

- `cv2.STITCHER_OK`
- `cv2.STITCHER_ERR_NEED_MORE_IMGS`
- `cv2.STITCHER_ERR_HOMOGRAPHY_EST_FAIL`
- `cv2.STITCHER_ERR_CAMERA_PARAMS_ADJUST_FAIL`

The first value means the panorama was successfully created. The other values tell you that the panorama wasn't composed and gives you some hints about possible reasons.

The success of the stitching depends on the input images. They should have overlapping regions. The more overlapping areas there are, the easier it is for the algorithm to match the frames and correctly map them to the final panorama. Also, it's better to have photos from a camera that rotates. Small movements of the camera are fine, but undesirable.

You will see images similar to the following figure after executing the code:

As you can see in the figure, reflections didn't spoil the final result: the algorithm successfully handled this situation. This result was achieved because the images have large overlapping areas and many regions with rich texture. In case of textureless objects, the reflections may hinder.

Denoising a photo using non-local means algorithms

In this recipe, you will learn how to remove noise from images using non-local means algorithms. This functionality is useful when photos suffer from excessive noise and it's necessary to remove it to get a better looking image.

Getting ready

Before you proceed with this recipe, you need to install the OpenCV version 3.3 (or greater) Python API package.

How to do it

You need to complete the following steps:

1. Import the necessary modules:

```
import cv2
import numpy as np
import matplotlib.pyplot as plt
```

2. Load the test image:

```
img = cv2.imread('../data/Lena.png')
```

3. Generate a random Gaussian noise:

```
noise = 30 * np.random.randn(*img.shape)
img = np.uint8(np.clip(img + noise, 0, 255))
```

4. Perform denoising using the non-local means algorithm:

```
denoised_nlm = cv2.fastNlMeansDenoisingColored(img, None, 10)
```

5. Visualize the results:

```
plt.figure(0, figsize=(10,6))
plt.subplot(121)
plt.axis('off')
plt.title('original')
plt.imshow(img[:,:,[2,1,0]])
plt.subplot(122)
plt.axis('off')
plt.title('denoised')
plt.imshow(denoised_nlm[:,:,[2,1,0]])
plt.show()
```

How it works

The non-local means algorithm is implemented in OpenCV by a family of functions: `cv2.fastNlMeansDenoising`, `cv2.fastNlMeansDenoisingColored`, `cv2.fastNlMeansMulti`, and `cv2.fastNlMeansDenoisingColoredMulti`. These functions take either one image or multiple images, gray-scale or color. In this recipe, we used the `cv2.fastNlMeansDenoisingColored` function, which takes a single BGR image and returns a denoised one. The function takes a few parameters, among them the parameter h, which stands for denoising strength; higher values leads to less noise, but a more smoothed image. The other parameters specify non-local means algorithms parameters such as template pattern size and search window space (named correspondingly).

The following image shows the expected results:

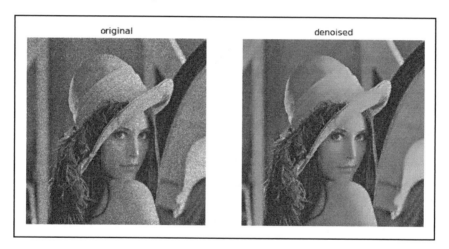

Constructing an HDR image

Almost all modern cameras and even phones have a magical *HDR* mode, and it produces a truly miraculous result—photos don't contain under- or overexposed areas. **HDR (High Dynamic Range)**, and you can reproduce such a result in OpenCV! This recipe tells you about HDR imaging functions and how to use them properly.

Getting ready

Before you proceed with this recipe, you need to install the OpenCV version 3.3 (or greater) Python API package.

How to do it

You need to complete the following steps:

1. Import the necessary modules:

```
import cv2
import numpy as np
```

2. Load the images and exposure times:

```
imgs_names = ['33', '100', '179', '892', '1560', '2933']

exp_times = []
images = []

for name in imgs_names:
    exp_times.append(1/float(name))
    images.append(cv2.imread('../data/hdr/%s.jpg' % name,
cv2.IMREAD_COLOR))

exp_times = np.array(exp_times).astype(np.float32)
```

3. Recover the CRF:

```
calibrate = cv2.createCalibrateDebevec()
response = calibrate.process(images, exp_times)
```

4. Compute an HDR image:

```
merge_debevec = cv2.createMergeDebevec()
hdr = merge_debevec.process(images, exp_times, response)
```

5. Turn the HDR image into a **Low Dynamic Range** (**LDR**) image to be able to display it:

```
tonemap = cv2.createTonemapDurand(2.4)
ldr = tonemap.process(hdr)

ldr = cv2.normalize(ldr, None, 0, 1, cv2.NORM_MINMAX)

cv2.imshow('ldr', ldr)
cv2.waitKey()
cv2.destroyAllWindows()
```

6. Apply this technique to merge images with various exposures:

```
merge_mertens = cv2.createMergeMertens()
fusion = merge_mertens.process(images)

fusion = cv2.normalize(fusion, None, 0, 1, cv2.NORM_MINMAX)

cv2.imshow('fusion', fusion)
cv2.waitKey()
cv2.destroyAllWindows()
```

How it works

First, you need to have a set of images with different known exposure times. Modern cameras store a lot of information including exposure time in image files, so it's worth checking the image's properties.

Computing an HDR image starts with recovering **CRF** (**Camera Response Function**), which is a mapping between real intensity and the pixel's intensity (which is in the [0, 255] range) for each color channel. Usually it's non-linear, and makes it impossible to simply combine images with different exposures. It can be done by creating an instance of the calibrate algorithm with cv2.createCalibrateDebevec. When the calibration instance is created, you need to invoke its process method and pass an array of images and an array of exposure times. The process method returns CRF of our camera.

The next step is creating an HDR image. To do this, we should get an instance of the photos merging algorithm by calling cv2.createMergeDebevec. When the object is constructed, we need to call its process method and pass images, exposure times, and CRF as arguments. As a result, we get an HDR image, which can't be displayed with imshow, but can be saved in the .hdr format with imwrite and viewed in special tools.

Now we need to display our HDR image. To do this, we need to correctly squeeze its dynamic range to 8 bits. This process is called tonemapping. To perform this process, you need to build a tonemapping object with `cv2.createTonemapDurand` and call its `process` function. This function accepts an HDR image and a returns floating point image.

There's also an alternative way to merge photos with different exposures. You need to create another algorithm instance with the `cv2.createMergeMertens` function. The resulting object has the `process` method, which merges our images—just pass them as an argument. The result of the function work is a merged image.

After launching the code from this recipe, you see images similar to the ones shown in the following figure:

In the top row of the figure are the two original images with different exposures: the left one with a long exposure time, and the right one with a short exposure time. As a result, we can see both the desk lamp labels near the bulb and the QR code. The bottom row contains the results for two approaches from the recipe's code—in both cases, we can see all the details.

Removing defects from a photo with image inpainting

Sometimes, photo images have defects. This is especially the case for old photos that have been scanned: they may have scratches, spots, and stains. All these imperfections hinder enjoyment of the photo. The procedure of reconstructing parts of an image based on their surroundings is called inpainting, and OpenCV has an implementation of this algorithm. Here, we'll review ways of exploiting this OpenCV functionality.

Getting ready

Before you proceed with this recipe, you need to install the OpenCV version 3.3 (or greater) Python API package.

How to do it

You need to complete the following steps:

1. Import the necessary modules:

```
import cv2
import numpy as np
```

2. Define a class that encapsulates mask creation:

```
class MaskCreator:
    def __init__(self, image, mask):
        self.prev_pt = None
        self.image = image
        self.mask = mask
        self.dirty = False
        self.show()
        cv2.setMouseCallback('mask', self.mouse_callback)

    def show(self):
        cv2.imshow('mask', self.image)

    def mouse_callback(self, event, x, y, flags, param):
        pt = (x, y)
        if event == cv2.EVENT_LBUTTONDOWN:
            self.prev_pt = pt
        elif event == cv2.EVENT_LBUTTONUP:
            self.prev_pt = None

        if self.prev_pt and flags & cv2.EVENT_FLAG_LBUTTON:
            cv2.line(self.image, self.prev_pt, pt, (127,)*3, 5)
            cv2.line(self.mask, self.prev_pt, pt, 255, 5)
            self.dirty = True
            self.prev_pt = pt
            self.show()
```

3. Load an image, create its defect version and a mask, apply inpaint agorithms, and display the results:

```
img = cv2.imread('../data/Lena.png')

defect_img = img.copy()
mask = np.zeros(img.shape[:2], np.uint8)
m_creator = MaskCreator(defect_img, mask)

while True:
    k = cv2.waitKey()
    if k == 27:
        break
    if k == ord('a'):
        res_telea = cv2.inpaint(defect_img, mask, 3,
cv2.INPAINT_TELEA)
        res_ns = cv2.inpaint(defect_img, mask, 3, cv2.INPAINT_NS)
        cv2.imshow('TELEA vs NS', np.hstack((res_telea, res_ns)))
    if k == ord('c'):
        defect_img[:] = img
        mask[:] = 0
        m_creator.show()
cv2.destroyAllWindows()
```

How it works

To inpaint images in OpenCV, you need to use the cv2.inpaint function. It accepts four arguments:

- **Image with defects**: It has to be an 8-bit colorful or grayscale one
- **Mask for defects**: It has to be an 8-bit single channel one and be the same size as the image in the first argument
- **Neighborhood radius**: The size of the area around a *damaged* pixel, which should be used in computing its color
- **Inpainting mode**: Type of the algorithm of inpainting

Mask for defects should contain non-zero values for pixels on the original image, which need to be recovered. Neighborhood radius is a range of pixels around the algorithm that it considers during inpainting; it should have a small value to prevent dramatic blurring effects. Inpainting mode has to be one of the following values: `cv2.INPAINT_TELEA` or `cv2.INPAINT_NS`. Depending on the circumstances, one algorithm may work slightly better than the other and vise versa, so it's better to compare the results of both algorithms and choose the best. `cv2.inpaint` returns the resulting repaired image.

As a result of launching the code, you will see similar images:

As you can see in the preceding figure, the easiest defects to recover are small or almost textureless areas, which is no surprise. Inpainting algorithms don't implement any magic, so there are visible yet colored imperfections in the complicated parts of the images.

9
Multiple View Geometry

This chapter covers the following recipes:

- Pinhole camera model calibration
- Fisheye camera model calibration
- Stereo rig calibration - estimation of extrinsics
- Distorting and undistorting points
- Removing lens distortion effects from an image
- Restoring a 3D point from two observations through triangulation
- Finding a relative camera-object pose through the PnP algorithm
- Aligning two views through stereo rectification
- Epipolar geometry - computing fundamental and essential matrices
- Essential matrix decomposition into rotation and translation
- Estimating disparity maps for stereo images
- Special case 2-view geometry - estimating homography transformation
- Planar scene - decomposing homography into rotation and translation
- Rotational camera cas - estimating camera rotation from homography

Introduction

Projection of a 3D scene onto a 2D image, in other words using a camera, eliminates information about how far scene objects are from the photographer. But in some cases, 3D information can be restored. This requires not only knowing information about objects or camera configuration, but also having a camera's intrinsic parameters. This chapter sheds light on all the necessary steps for getting 3D information for 2D images, from camera calibration to 3D object position reconstruction and depth map retrieval.

Pinhole camera model calibration

The pinhole camera model is the simplest mathematical model as well as others, yet it can be applied to a lot of real photography devices. This recipe tells you how to calibrate your camera, for example, finding its intrinsic parameters and distortion coefficients.

Getting ready

Before you proceed with this recipe, you need to install the OpenCV (version 3.3 or greater) Python API package.

How to do it

You need to complete the following steps:

1. Import the necessary modules:

```
import cv2
import numpy as np
```

2. Capture frames from the camera, detect a chessboard pattern on each frame, and accumulate the frames and corners until we have a big enough number of samples:

```
cap = cv2.VideoCapture(0)

pattern_size = (10, 7)

samples = []

while True:
    ret, frame = cap.read()
    if not ret:
        break
    res, corners = cv2.findChessboardCorners(frame, pattern_size)
    img_show = np.copy(frame)
    cv2.drawChessboardCorners(img_show, pattern_size, corners, res)
    cv2.putText(img_show, 'Samples captured: %d' % len(samples),
(0,
    40),
              cv2.FONT_HERSHEY_SIMPLEX, 1.0, (0, 255, 0), 2)
    cv2.imshow('chessboard', img_show)
```

```
wait_time = 0 if res else 30
k = cv2.waitKey(wait_time)
if k == ord('s') and res:
    samples.append((cv2.cvtColor(frame, cv2.COLOR_BGR2GRAY),
    corners))
elif k == 27:
    break

cap.release()
cv2.destroyAllWindows()
```

3. Refine all the detected corner points using `cv2.cornerSubPix`:

```
criteria = (cv2.TERM_CRITERIA_EPS + cv2.TERM_CRITERIA_MAX_ITER, 30,
1e-3)

for i in range(len(samples)):
    img, corners = samples[i]
    corners = cv2.cornerSubPix(img, corners, (10, 10), (-1,-1),
criteria)
```

4. Find the camera's intrinsic parameters by passing all refined corner points to
   `cv2.calibrateCamera`:

```
pattern_points = np.zeros((np.prod(pattern_size), 3), np.float32)
pattern_points[:, :2] = np.indices(pattern_size).T.reshape(-1, 2)

images, corners = zip(*samples)

pattern_points = [pattern_points]*len(corners)

rms, camera_matrix, dist_coefs, rvecs, tvecs = \
    cv2.calibrateCamera(pattern_points, corners, images[0].shape,
    None, None)

np.save('camera_mat.npy', camera_matrix)
np.save('dist_coefs.npy', dist_coefs)
```

How it works

Camera calibration aims to find two sets of intrinsic parameters: the camera matrix and
distortion coefficients. The camera matrix determines how coordinates of 3D points are
mapped onto dimensionless pixels coordinates in the image, but actual image lenses also
distort an image so straight lines are transformed into curves. Distortion coefficients allow
you to eliminate such warps.

The whole camera calibration process can be divided into three stages:

- Gathering a decent amount of data such as, images and detected chessboard patterns
- Refining chessboard corners coordinates
- Optimizing camera parameters to match them with observed distortions and projections

To gather data for camera calibration, you need to detect a chessboard pattern of a certain size and accumulate pairs of images and coordinates of the found corners. As you know from the *Detecting chessboard and circles grid patterns* recipe from Chapter 4, *Object Detection and Machine Learning,* cv2.findChessboardCorners implements chessboard corner detection. For more information, see Chapter 4, *Object Detection and Machine Learning*. It's worth mentioning that corners on the chessboard are the ones formed by two black squares, and the pattern size you pass in cv2.findChessboardCorners should be the same as you have in the real chessboard pattern. The number of samples and their distribution along the field of view is also very important. In practical cases, 50 to 100 samples is enough.

The next step is refining the corner's coordinates. This stage is necessary due to the fact that cv2.findChessboardCorners does not give a very accurate result, so we need to find the actual corner positions. cv2.cornerSubPix gives precision to corner coordinates with sub-pixel accuracy. It accepts the following arguments:

- Grayscale images
- Coarse coordinates of detected corners
- Size of the refine region to find a more accurate corner position
- Size of the zone in the center of the refine region to ignore
- Criteria to stop the refining process

Coarse coordinates of corners are the ones returned by cv2.findChessboardCorners. The refine region should be small, but it should include the actual position of the corner; otherwise, the coarse corner is returned. The size of the zone to ignore should be smaller than the refine region and can be disabled by passing (-1, -1) as its value. The stop criteria can be one of the following types, cv2.TERM_CRITERIA_EPS or cv2.TERM_CRITERIA_MAX_ITER, or a combinationof the two. cv2.TERM_CRITERIA_EPS determines the difference in previous and next corner positions. If the actual difference is less than the one defined, the process will be stopped. cv2.TERM_CRITERIA_MAX_ITER determines the maximum number of iterations. cv2.cornerSubPix returns the same number of corners with refined coordinates.

Once we have refined the corner's positions, it's time to find the camera's parameters. `cv2.calibrateCamera` solves this problem. You need to pass a few parameters to this function, and these are listed as follows:

- Object points coordinates for all samples
- Corners points coordinates for all samples
- Shape of the images in (width, height) format
- Two arrays to save translation and rotation vectors (can be set to None)
- Flags and stop criteria (both have default values)

Object points are 3D coordinates of chessboard corners in a chessboard coordinate system. Because we use the same pattern for each frame, the 3D coordinates of the corners are the same and, because we use equidistantly distributed corners, 3D coordinates are also equidistantly distributed on the plane (z=0 for all points). The actual distance between corners doesn't matter because the camera eliminates the z coordinate (how far objects are from the camera), so it can be a smaller but closer pattern, or a bigger but farther one—the image is the same. `cv2.calibrateCamera` returns five values: the mean reprojection error for all samples, the camera matrix, distortion coefficients, rotation, and translation vectors for all samples. The reprojection error is the difference between a corner in the image and the projection of a 3D point of the corner. Ideally, the projection of the corner and its original position in the image should be the same, but there is a difference due to the noise. This difference is measured in pixels. The smaller this difference is, the better the calibration is done. The camera matrix has a shape of 3x3. The number of distortion coefficients depends on the flags and it equals 5 by default.

As a result of executing this code you will see the following image:

Fisheye camera model calibration

If your camera has a wide view angle and, as a consequence, strong distortions, you need to use the fisheye camera model. OpenCV provides functions to work with the fisheye camera model. Let's review how to calibrate such a camera type in OpenCV.

Getting ready

Before you proceed with this recipe, you need to install the OpenCV version 3.3 (or greater) Python API package.

How to do it

You need to complete the following steps:

1. Import the necessary modules:

```
import cv2
import numpy as np
```

2. Capture frames from the camera, detect a chessboard pattern on each frame, and accumulate the frames and corners until we have a big enough number of samples:

```
cap = cv2.VideoCapture(0)

pattern_size = (10, 7)

samples = []

while True:
    ret, frame = cap.read()
    if not ret:
        break
    res, corners = cv2.findChessboardCorners(frame, pattern_size)
    img_show = np.copy(frame)
    cv2.drawChessboardCorners(img_show, pattern_size, corners, res)
    cv2.putText(img_show, 'Samples captured: %d' % len(samples),
(0, 40),
                cv2.FONT_HERSHEY_SIMPLEX, 1.0, (0, 255, 0), 2)
    cv2.imshow('chessboard', img_show)
    wait_time = 0 if res else 30
```

```
        k = cv2.waitKey(wait_time)
        if k == ord('s') and res:
            samples.append((cv2.cvtColor(frame, cv2.COLOR_BGR2GRAY),
corners))
        elif k == 27:
            break

cap.release()
cv2.destroyAllWindows()
```

3. Refine all the detected corner points using `cv2.cornerSubPix`:

```
criteria = (cv2.TERM_CRITERIA_EPS + cv2.TERM_CRITERIA_MAX_ITER, 30,
1e-3)

for i in range(len(samples)):
    img, corners = samples[i]
    corners = cv2.cornerSubPix(img, corners, (10, 10), (-1,-1),
criteria)
```

4. Import the necessary modules, open an input image, and copy it:

```
pattern_points = np.zeros((1, np.prod(pattern_size), 3),
np.float32)
pattern_points[0, :, :2] = np.indices(pattern_size).T.reshape(-1,
2)

images, corners = zip(*samples)

pattern_points = [pattern_points]*len(corners)

print(len(pattern_points), pattern_points[0].shape,
pattern_points[0].dtype)
print(len(corners), corners[0].shape, corners[0].dtype)

rms, camera_matrix, dis t_coefs, rvecs, tvecs = \
    cv2.fisheye.calibrate(pattern_points, corners, images[0].shape,
None, None)

np.save('camera_mat.npy', camera_matrix)
np.save('dist_coefs.npy', dist_coefs)
```

How it works

The camera calibration procedures for both fisheye and pinhole cameras are basically the same, so it's strongly recommended to go through the *Pinhole camera model calibration* recipe, because all the main steps and recommendations from the pinhole camera case are applicable for the fisheye camera too.

Let's review the key difference. To calibrate the fisheye model camera, you need to use the `cv2.fisheye.calibrate` function. It accepts the same arguments as `cv2.calibrateCamera`, but this function supports only its own values for flags. Fortunately, this argument has a default value.

As a result of executing this code, you will see an image similar to the following:

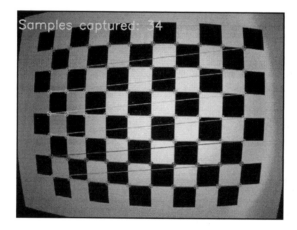

Stereo rig calibration - estimation of extrinsics

In this recipe, you will learn how to calibrate a stereo pair, that is, an estimate relative rotation and translation between two cameras using the photos of a calibration pattern. This functionality is used when you're dealing with stereo cameras—you need to know the rig parameters to be able to reconstruct 3D information about the scene.

Getting ready

Before you proceed with this recipe, you need to install the OpenCV version 3.3 (or greater) Python API package.

How to do it

You need to complete the following steps:

1. Import the necessary modules:

```
import cv2
import glob
import numpy as np
```

2. Set the pattern size and prepare lists with images:

```
PATTERN_SIZE = (9, 6)
left_imgs =
list(sorted(glob.glob('../data/stereo/case1/left*.png')))
right_imgs =
list(sorted(glob.glob('../data/stereo/case1/right*.png')))
assert len(left_imgs) == len(right_imgs)
```

3. Find the chessboard points:

```
criteria = (cv2.TERM_CRITERIA_EPS + cv2.TERM_CRITERIA_MAX_ITER, 30,
1e-3)
left_pts, right_pts = [], []
img_size = None

for left_img_path, right_img_path in zip(left_imgs, right_imgs):
    left_img = cv2.imread(left_img_path, cv2.IMREAD_GRAYSCALE)
    right_img = cv2.imread(right_img_path, cv2.IMREAD_GRAYSCALE)
    if img_size is None:
        img_size = (left_img.shape[1], left_img.shape[0])
    res_left, corners_left = cv2.findChessboardCorners(left_img,
PATTERN_SIZE)
    res_right, corners_right = cv2.findChessboardCorners(right_img,
PATTERN_SIZE)
    corners_left = cv2.cornerSubPix(left_img, corners_left, (10,
10), (-1,-1),
                                    criteria)
    corners_right = cv2.cornerSubPix(right_img, corners_right, (10,
10), (-1,-1),
```

```
                                                    criteria)
    left_pts.append(corners_left)
    right_pts.append(corners_right)
```

4. Prepare the calibration pattern points:

```
pattern_points = np.zeros((np.prod(PATTERN_SIZE), 3), np.float32)
pattern_points[:, :2] = np.indices(PATTERN_SIZE).T.reshape(-1, 2)
pattern_points = [pattern_points] * len(left_imgs)
```

5. Estimate the stereo pair parameters:

```
err, Kl, Dl, Kr, Dr, R, T, E, F = cv2.stereoCalibrate(
    pattern_points, left_pts, right_pts, None, None, None, None,
img_size, flags=0)
```

6. Report the calibration's results:

```
print('Left camera:')
print(Kl)
print('Left camera distortion:')
print(Dl)
print('Right camera:')
print(Kr)
print('Right camera distortion:')
print(Dr)
print('Rotation matrix:')
print(R)
print('Translation:')
print(T)
```

How it works

To calibrate a stereo pair using OpenCV, one must capture a few photos of a calibration pattern simultaneously from both cameras. In our case, we used a 9x6 chessboard. We used the `cv2.findChessboardCorners` function to find corners of the board which we will use for rig parameters estimation. We also need calibration pattern points in its local coordinate system. Since we know the size of the pattern and its shape, we can explicitly construct the list of points—`pattern_points`. Note that the units used here will be used for the translation vector between two cameras.

The calibration itself is performed in the `cv2.stereoCalibrate` function. As input, it takes a list of image points and a list of pattern points. You can also specify initial guesses for calibration parameters, and specify which parameters you want to refine and which ones you want to keep unchanged. The function returns a calibration error in pixels, first camera parameters, first camera distortion coefficients, second camera parameters, second camera distortion coefficients, rotation and translation between cameras, and essential and fundamental matrices.

The following is the expected output:

```
Left camera:
[[ 534.36681752    0.          341.45684657]
 [   0.          534.29616718  235.72519106]
 [   0.            0.            1.        ]]
Left camera distortion:
[[ -2.79470900e-01   4.71876981e-02   1.39511507e-03  -1.64158448e-04
     7.01729203e-02]]
Right camera:
[[ 537.88729748    0.          327.29925115]
 [   0.          537.43063947  250.10021993]
 [   0.            0.            1.        ]]
Right camera distortion:
[[-0.28990693  0.12537789 -0.00040656  0.00053461 -0.03844589]]
Rotation matrix:
[[ 0.99998995  0.00355598  0.00273003]
 [-0.00354058  0.99997791 -0.00562461]
 [-0.00274997  0.00561489  0.99998046]]
Translation:
[[-3.33161159]
 [ 0.03706722]
 [-0.00420814]]
```

Distorting and undistorting points

Camera lenses produce distortions of an image. The calibration process aims to find parameters of these distortions, as well as the parameters of 3D points projection onto an image plane. This recipe tells you how to apply a camera matrix and distortion coefficients to get undistorted image points and distort them back.

Getting ready

Before you proceed with this recipe, you need to install the OpenCV version 3.3 (or greater) Python API package.

How to do it

You need to complete the following steps:

1. Import the necessary modules:

   ```
   import cv2
   import numpy as np
   ```

2. Load the camera matrix and distortion coefficients for our camera:

   ```
   camera_matrix = np.load('../data/pinhole_calib/camera_mat.npy')
   dist_coefs = np.load('../data/pinhole_calib/dist_coefs.npy')
   ```

3. Open a photo of a chessboard taken by the camera, and find and refine the corners:

   ```
   img = cv2.imread('../data/pinhole_calib/img_00.png')
   pattern_size = (10, 7)
   res, corners = cv2.findChessboardCorners(img, pattern_size)
   criteria = (cv2.TERM_CRITERIA_EPS + cv2.TERM_CRITERIA_MAX_ITER, 30,
   1e-3)
   corners = cv2.cornerSubPix(cv2.cvtColor(img, cv2.COLOR_BGR2GRAY),
                             corners, (10, 10), (-1,-1), criteria)
   ```

4. Undistort the corner's coordinates and turn them into 3D points:

   ```
   h_corners = cv2.undistortPoints(corners, camera_matrix, dist_coefs)
   h_corners = np.c_[h_corners.squeeze(), np.ones(len(h_corners))]
   ```

5. Project the 3D coordinates of the corners to the image without applying distortion:

   ```
   img_pts, _ = cv2.projectPoints(h_corners, (0, 0, 0), (0, 0, 0),
   camera_matrix, None)

   for c in corners:
       cv2.circle(img, tuple(c[0]), 10, (0, 255, 0), 2)

   for c in img_pts.squeeze().astype(np.float32):
   ```

```
        cv2.circle(img, tuple(c), 5, (0, 0, 255), 2)

    cv2.imshow('undistorted corners', img)
    cv2.waitKey()
    cv2.destroyAllWindows()
```

6. Project the 3D coordinates of the corners to the image and apply lenses distortion:

```
    img_pts, _ = cv2.projectPoints(h_corners, (0, 0, 0), (0, 0, 0),
    camera_matrix, dist_coefs)

    for c in img_pts.squeeze().astype(np.float32):
        cv2.circle(img, tuple(c), 2, (255, 255, 0), 2)

    cv2.imshow('reprojected corners', img)
    cv2.waitKey()
    cv2.destroyAllWindows()
```

How it works

cv2.undistortPoints finds homogeneous coordinates for points in the image. This function removes lens distortion and unprojects the points so that they are in dimensionless coordinates. This function accepts the following arguments: an array of 2D points in the image, a 3x3 camera matrix, a set of distortion coefficients, an object to store the result, and rectification and projection matrices, which are used in the stereo vision and aren't relevant now. The last three arguments are optional. cv2.undistortPoints returns the set of undistorted and unprojected points.

The points returned by cv2.undistortPoints are *ideal*—their coordinates are dimensionless and aren't distorted by lenses. If we need to project them back, we need to turn them into 3D points. To do so, we just need to add the third Z coordinate to each point. Because the coordinates of the points are homogeneous, Z is equal to 1.

When we have 3D points and want to project them onto the image, cv2.projectPoints comes into play. In a general case, this function takes 3D coordinates of points in some coordinate system, rotates and translates them to get the coordinates in the camera coordinate system, and then applies the camera matrix and distortion coefficients to find projections of the points onto the image plane.

The arguments for `cv2.>projectPoints` are: an array of 3D points in some local coordinate system, rotation and translation vectors of a transition from the local coordinate system to the camera coordinate system, a 3x3 camera matrix, an array of distortion coefficients, an object to store the resulting points, an object to store Jacobian values, and the value of the aspect ratio. Again, the last three parameters are optional and can be omitted. This function returns the projected and distorted coordinates of the 3D points and Jacobian values. If you want to get the positions of points without lenses distortion, you can pass None as the value of the distortion coefficients array.

As a result of executing this code, you will see an image similar to the following:

Green circles in the figure are the original locations of chessboard corners; the red ones are the projected coordinates of corners, but without lens distortion; light blue points are projected coordinates after distortion—they're exactly at the center of the green circles. Also, as you may notice, green and light blue circles aren't laid on the straight lines, but red ones are. This is the effect of lense distortion. You may also be able to notice that, for corners far from the image's center, the difference between red and light blue circle coordinates is noticeable, though circles near the image center are almost identical. This happens due to the degree of lens distortion, and this depends on how far the point is from the lens center.

Removing lens distortion effects from an image

If you need to remove lens distortion effects from a whole image, you need to use dense remapping. Essentially, the undistortion algorithm warps and compresses the image in a way to compensate for lens effects, but compression leads to blank regions appearing. This recipe tells you how to undistort images and remove empty regions from the undistorted image.

Getting ready

Before you proceed with this recipe, you need to install the OpenCV version 3.3 (or greater) Python API package.

How to do it

You need to complete the following steps:

1. Import the necessary modules:

    ```
    import cv2
    import numpy as np
    ```

2. Load the camera matrix and distortion coefficients for our camera, and a photo, that was taken by the same camera:

    ```
    camera_matrix = np.load('../data/pinhole_calib/camera_mat.npy')
    dist_coefs = np.load('../data/pinhole_calib/dist_coefs.npy')
    img = cv2.imread('../data/pinhole_calib/img_00.png')
    ```

3. Undistort the image with `cv2.undistort`—the empty regions will appear in the image:

    ```
    ud_img = cv2.undistort(img, camera_matrix, dist_coefs)

    cv2.imshow('undistorted image', ud_img)
    cv2.waitKey(0)

    cv2.destroyAllWindows()
    ```

4. Eliminate the empty regions by computing the optimal camera matrix and applying it to get the undistorted image without black regions:

```
opt_cam_mat, valid_roi =
cv2.getOptimalNewCameraMatrix(camera_matrix, dist_coefs,
img.shape[:2][::-1], 0)

ud_img = cv2.undistort(img, camera_matrix, dist_coefs, None,
opt_cam_mat)

cv2.imshow('undistorted image', ud_img)
cv2.waitKey(0)

cv2.destroyAllWindows()
```

How it works

cv2.undistort removes lenses distortion from the image. It takes the following arguments: the image to undistort, the camera matrix, the distortion coefficients array, an object to store the undistorted image, and an optimal camera matrix. The last two arguments are optional. The function returns the undistorted image. If you missed the last parameter of cv2.undistort, the resulting image will contain empty (of black color) regions. The optimal camera matrix argument allows you to get the image without these artifacts, but we need a way to compute this optimal camera matrix, and OpenCV serves it.

cv2.getOptimalNewCameraMatrix creates an optimal camera matrix to get rid of black regions on the undistorted image. It takes the camera matrix, distortion coefficients, the original image size in (width, height) format, the alpha factor, the resulting image size (again in (width, height) format), and a Boolean flag to set the principal camera point of the camera in the center of the output image. The last two arguments are optional. The alpha factor is a double value in range [0, 1] and it shows the degree of removing empty regions: 0 means complete removal and, as a consequence, loss of some portion of image pixels, while 1 means preserving all the image pixels along with the empty regions. If you don't set the output image size, it is set to the same as the input image's dimensions.

After launching the code from the recipe, you will see images similar to the following:

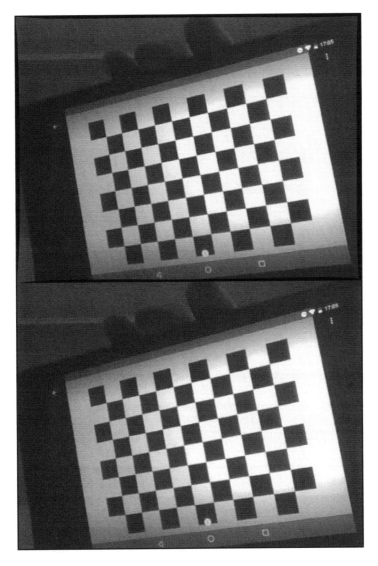

As you can see, the upper image has black regions near the border and the lower one doesn't.

Restoring a 3D point from two observations through triangulation

In this recipe, you will learn how to reconstruct 3D point coordinates given observations in two views. This is a building block for many higher level 3D reconstruction algorithms and SLAM systems.

Getting ready

Before you proceed with this recipe, you need to install the OpenCV version 3.3 (or greater) Python API package.

How to do it

You need to complete the following steps:

1. Import the necessary modules.

   ```
   import cv2
   import numpy as np
   ```

2. Generate the test camera's projection matrices:

   ```
   P1 = np.eye(3, 4, dtype=np.float32)
   P2 = np.eye(3, 4, dtype=np.float32)
   P2[0, 3] = -1
   ```

3. Generate the test points:

   ```
   N = 5
   points3d = np.empty((4, N), np.float32)
   points3d[:3, :] = np.random.randn(3, N)
   points3d[3, :] = 1
   ```

4. Project the 3D points into two views and add noise:

   ```
   points1 = P1 @ points3d
   points1 = points1[:2, :] / points1[2, :]
   points1[:2, :] += np.random.randn(2, N) * 1e-2

   points2 = P2 @ points3d
   ```

```
points2 = points2[:2, :] / points2[2, :]
points2[:2, :] += np.random.randn(2, N) * 1e-2
```

5. Reconstruct the points from noisy observations:

```
points3d_reconstr = cv2.triangulatePoints(P1, P2, points1, points2)
points3d_reconstr /= points3d_reconstr[3, :]
```

6. Print the results:

```
print('Original points')
print(points3d[:3].T)
print('Reconstructed points')
print(points3d_reconstr[:3].T)
```

How it works

We generate random points in the 3D space and project them into two test views. Then, we add noise to those observations and reconstruct points back in 3D using the OpenCV function `cv2.triangulatePoints`. As input, the function takes observations from two cameras and camera projection matrices (projective mapping from the world coordinate frame to a view coordinate frame) for each view. It returns the reconstructed points in the world coordinate frame.

The following are the possible results:

```
Original points
[[ 0.48245686 -2.05779004  1.3458606 ]
 [-0.18333936 -1.00662899 -0.46047512]
 [-0.51193094 -0.54561883  0.20674749]
 [ 1.05258393 -1.55241323  0.60368073]
 [ 1.80103588 -0.83367926 -0.59293056]]
Reconstructed points
[[ 0.47777811 -2.05873108  1.3407315 ]
 [-0.17389734 -0.99433696 -0.45361272]
 [-0.51100874 -0.54552656  0.20692034]
 [ 1.05780101 -1.54776227  0.60341281]
 [ 1.81407869 -0.83914387 -0.59897166]]
```

Finding a relative camera-object pose through the PnP algorithm

The camera removes information regarding how far away the object that is being photographed is. It may be a small but close object, or a big but far away one—the images may be the same—but by knowing the geometrical size of the object, we can compute the distance from it to the camera. In general, our knowledge about an object's geometry is the positions of some set of 3D points in an object's local coordinate system. And usually, we want to know not only the distance between the camera and the object's local coordinate system, but also how the object is oriented. This task can be successfully done with OpenCV. This recipe will show you how to find a 6-DOF (degrees of freedom) position of an object if we know the configuration of its 3D points and their corresponding 2D projections on the image.

Getting ready

Before you proceed with this recipe, you need to install the OpenCV version 3.3 (or greater) Python API package.

How to do it

You need to complete the following steps:

1. Import the necessary modules:

```
import cv2
import numpy as np
```

2. Load the camera matrix, distortion coefficients, and a photo of the object taken by the camera:

```
camera_matrix = np.load('../data/pinhole_calib/camera_mat.npy')
dist_coefs = np.load('../data/pinhole_calib/dist_coefs.npy')
img = cv2.imread('../data/pinhole_calib/img_00.png')
```

3. Detect the object points in the image, in our case, chessboard corners:

```
pattern_size = (10, 7)
res, corners = cv2.findChessboardCorners(img, pattern_size)
criteria = (cv2.TERM_CRITERIA_EPS + cv2.TERM_CRITERIA_MAX_ITER, 30,
```

```
1e-3)
corners = cv2.cornerSubPix(cv2.cvtColor(img, cv2.COLOR_BGR2GRAY),
                           corners, (10, 10), (-1,-1), criteria)
```

4. Create the configuration of 3D object points:

```
pattern_points = np.zeros((np.prod(pattern_size), 3), np.float32)
pattern_points[:, :2] = np.indices(pattern_size).T.reshape(-1, 2)
```

5. Find the object's position and orientation by using `cv2.solvePnP`:

```
ret, rvec, tvec = cv2.solvePnP(pattern_points, corners,
camera_matrix, dist_coefs,
                         None, None, False,
cv2.SOLVEPNP_ITERATIVE)
```

6. Project the object's points back to the image by applying the found rotation and translation. Draw the projected points:

```
img_points, _ = cv2.projectPoints(pattern_points, rvec, tvec,
camera_matrix, dist_coefs)

for c in img_points.squeeze():
    cv2.circle(img, tuple(c), 10, (0, 255, 0), 2)

cv2.imshow('points', img)
cv2.waitKey()

cv2.destroyAllWindows()
```

How it works

`cv2.solvePnP` is able to find the translation and rotation of the object by its 3D points in a local coordinate system and their 2D projections onto the image. It accepts a set of 3D points, a set of 2D points, a 3x3 camera matrix, distortion coefficients, the initial rotation and translation vectors (optional), a flag of whether to use the initial position and orientation, and the type of problem solver. The first two arguments should contain the same number of points. The type of solver may be one of many: `cv2.SOLVEPNP_ITERATIVE`, `cv2.SOLVEPNP_EPNP`, `cv2.SOLVEPNP_DLS`, and so on.

By default, `cv2.SOLVEPNP_ITERATIVE` is used and it gets decent results in many cases. `cv2.solvePnP` returns three values: a success flag, a rotation vector, and a translation vector. The success flag indicates that the problem has been solved correctly. The translation vector has the same units as the object's 3D local points. The rotation vector is returned in Rodrigues form: the direction of the vector means the axis around which the object is revolved, and the norm of the vector means the angle of rotation.

After launching the code from the recipe, it displays an image similar to the following:

Aligning two views through stereo rectification

In this recipe, you will learn how to rectify two images captured using a stereo camera with known parameters in such a way that, for the point (x_l, y_l) in the left image, the corresponding epipolar line in the right image is $y_r = y_l$ and vice versa. This greatly simplifies feature matching and dense stereo estimation algorithms.

Getting ready

Before you proceed with this recipe, you need to install the OpenCV version 3.3 (or greater) Python API package.

How to do it

You need to complete the following steps:

1. Import the necessary modules:

```
import cv2
import numpy as np
import matplotlib.pyplot as plt
```

2. Load the stereo rig calibration parameters:

```
data = np.load('../data/stereo/case1/stereo.npy').item()
Kl, Dl, Kr, Dr, R, T, img_size = data['Kl'], data['Dl'],
data['Kr'], data['Dr'], \
                                  data['R'], data['T'],
data['img_size']
```

3. Load the left and right test images:

```
left_img = cv2.imread('../data/stereo/case1/left14.png')
right_img = cv2.imread('../data/stereo/case1/right14.png')
```

4. Estimate the stereo rectification parameters:

```
R1, R2, P1, P2, Q, validRoi1, validRoi2 = cv2.stereoRectify(Kl, Dl,
Kr, Dr,
img_size, R, T)
```

5. Prepare the stereo rectification transformation maps:

```
xmap1, ymap1 = cv2.initUndistortRectifyMap(Kl, Dl, R1, Kl,
img_size, cv2.CV_32FC1)
xmap2, ymap2 = cv2.initUndistortRectifyMap(Kr, Dr, R2, Kr,
img_size, cv2.CV_32FC1)
```

6. Rectify the images:

```
left_img_rectified = cv2.remap(left_img, xmap1, ymap1,
cv2.INTER_LINEAR)
right_img_rectified = cv2.remap(right_img, xmap2, ymap2,
cv2.INTER_LINEAR)
```

7. Visualize the results:

```
plt.figure(0, figsize=(12,10))
plt.subplot(221)
plt.title('left original')
plt.imshow(left_img, cmap='gray')
plt.subplot(222)
plt.title('right original')
plt.imshow(right_img, cmap='gray')
plt.subplot(223)
plt.title('left rectified')
plt.imshow(left_img_rectified, cmap='gray')
plt.subplot(224)
plt.title('right rectified')
plt.imshow(right_img_rectified, cmap='gray')
plt.tight_layout()
plt.show()
```

How it works

We load stereo rig parameters estimated earlier from file. The rectification procedure itself estimates such camera transformations so that two separate image planes become the same plane afterwards. This greatly simplifies the epipolar geometry constraints and makes the job for all other stereo-related algorithms much easier.

The rectification transformation parameters are estimated using the cv2.stereoRectify function—it takes the stereo rig parameters and returns the rectification parameters: the first camera rotation, second camera rotation, first camera projection matrix, second camera projection matrix, disparity-to-depth mapping matrix, the first camera ROI where all the pixels are valid, and the second camera ROI where all the pixels are valid.

We only use the first two parameters; the first and second camera rotations are used to construct rectification transformation per-pixel maps using the cv2.initUndistortRectifyMap function. When the map has been computed once, it can then be used for any images captured using the stereo rig.

The expected results are shown as follows:

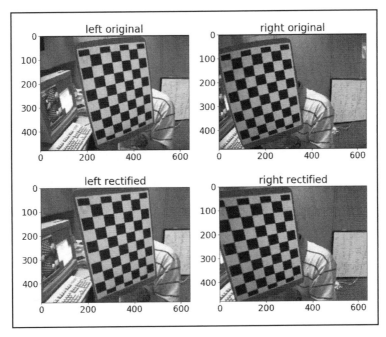

Epipolar geometry - computing fundamental and essential matrices

In this recipe, you will learn how to compute fundamental and essential matrices—the matrices comprising the epipolar geometry constraints in them. These matrices are useful for reconstructing stereo rig extrinsic parameters as well as other two-view vision algorithms.

Getting ready

Before you proceed with this recipe, you need to install the OpenCV version 3.3 (or greater) Python API package.

How to do it

You need to complete the following steps:

1. Import the necessary modules:

```
import cv2
import numpy as np
```

2. Load the left/right image point correspondences and the individual camera calibration parameters:

```
data = np.load('../data/stereo/case1/stereo.npy').item()
Kl, Kr, Dl, Dr, left_pts, right_pts, E_from_stereo, F_from_stereo = \
    data['Kl'], data['Kr'], data['Dl'], data['Dr'], \
    data['left_pts'], data['right_pts'], data['E'], data['F']
```

3. Stack the left and right point lists into arrays:

```
left_pts = np.vstack(left_pts)
right_pts = np.vstack(right_pts)
```

4. Get rid of lens distortions:

```
left_pts = cv2.undistortPoints(left_pts, Kl, Dl, P=Kl)
right_pts = cv2.undistortPoints(right_pts, Kr, Dr, P=Kr)
```

5. Estimate the fundamental matrix:

```
F, mask = cv2.findFundamentalMat(left_pts, right_pts, cv2.FM_LMEDS)
```

6. Estimate the essential matrix:

```
E = Kr.T @ F @ Kl
```

7. Print the results:

```
print('Fundamental matrix:')
print(F)
print('Essential matrix:')
print(E)
```

How it works

We used the `cv2.findFundamentalMat` function to estimate the fundamental matrix from left-right image point correspondences. This function supports a few different algorithms for fundamental matrix parameters estimation, such as `cv2.FM_7POINT` (7-point algorithm), `cv2.FM_8POINT` (8-point algorithm), `cv2.FM_LMEDS` (least-median approach), and `cv2.FM_RANSAC` (RANSAC-based approach). Two optional parameters specify the error threshold for RANSAC-based estimation algorithms and confidence levels for the least-median and RANSAC-based approaches.

The following are the expected results:

```
Fundamental matrix:
[[  1.60938825e-08  -2.23906409e-06  -2.53850603e-04]
 [  2.97226703e-06  -2.38236386e-07  -7.70276666e-02]
 [ -2.55190056e-04   7.69760820e-02   1.00000000e+00]]
Essential matrix:
[[  4.62585055e-03  -6.43487140e-01  -4.17486092e-01]
 [  8.53590806e-01  -6.84088948e-02  -4.08817705e+01]
 [  2.63679084e-01   4.07046349e+01  -2.20825664e-01]]
```

Essential matrix decomposition into rotation and translation

In this recipe, you will learn how to decompose essential matrices into two hypotheses about the relative rotation and translation vectors between two cameras in a stereo rig. This functionality is used when estimating stereo rig parameters.

Getting ready

Before you proceed with this recipe, you need to install the OpenCV version 3.3 (or greater) Python API package.

How to do it

You need to complete the following steps:

1. Import the necessary modules:

```
import cv2
import numpy as np
```

2. Load the precomputed essential matrix:

```
data = np.load('../data/stereo/case1/stereo.npy').item()
E = data['E']
```

3. Decompose the essential matrix into two possible rotations and translations:

```
R1, R2, T = cv2.decomposeEssentialMat(E)
```

4. Print the results:

```
print('Rotation 1:')
print(R1)
print('Rotation 2:')
print(R2)
print('Translation:')
print(T)
```

How it works

We use the OpenCV `cv2.decomposeEssentialMat` function, which takes an essential matrix as input and returns two candidates for rotation between cameras and one translation vector candidate. Note that since the translation vector can only be recovered up to a scale, it's returned in normalized form—unit length.

The following are the expected results:

```
Rotation 1:
[[ 0.99981105 -0.01867927  0.00538031]
 [-0.01870903 -0.99980965  0.00553437]
 [ 0.00527591 -0.00563399 -0.99997021]]
Rotation 2:
[[ 0.99998995  0.00355598  0.00273003]
 [-0.00354058  0.99997791 -0.00562461]
 [-0.00274997  0.00561489  0.99998046]]
Translation:
```

```
[[ 0.99993732]
 [-0.01112522]
 [ 0.00126302]]
```

Estimating disparity maps for stereo images

In this recipe, you will learn how to compute a disparity map from two rectified images. This functionality is useful in many computer vision applications where you need to recover information about depth in a scene, for example, collision avoidance in advanced driver assistance applications.

Getting ready

Before you proceed with this recipe, you need to install the OpenCV version 3.3 (or greater) Python API package.

How to do it

You need to complete the following steps:

1. Import the necessary modules:

```
import cv2
import numpy as np
```

2. Load the left and right rectified images:

```
left_img = cv2.imread('../data/stereo/left.png')
right_img = cv2.imread('../data/stereo/right.png')
```

3. Compute the disparity map using the stereo block matching algorithm:

```
stereo_bm = cv2.StereoBM_create(32)
dispmap_bm = stereo_bm.compute(cv2.cvtColor(left_img,
cv2.COLOR_BGR2GRAY),
                               cv2.cvtColor(right_img,
cv2.COLOR_BGR2GRAY))
```

4. Compute the disparity map using the stereo semi-global block matching algorithm:

```
stereo_sgbm = cv2.StereoSGBM_create(0, 32)
dispmap_sgbm = stereo_sgbm.compute(left_img, right_img)
```

5. Visualize the results:

```
plt.figure(figsize=(12,10))
plt.subplot(221)
plt.title('left')
plt.imshow(left_img[:,:,[2,1,0]])
plt.subplot(222)
plt.title('right')
plt.imshow(right_img[:,:,[2,1,0]])
plt.subplot(223)
plt.title('BM')
plt.imshow(dispmap_bm, cmap='gray')
plt.subplot(224)
plt.title('SGBM')
plt.imshow(dispmap_sgbm, cmap='gray')
plt.show()
```

How it works

We use two different algorithms for disparity maps calculation—block matching and semi-global block matching. After the map estimation object is instantiated using either `cv2.StereoBM_create` or `cv2.StereoSGBM_create` (where we specify maximum possible disparity), we call the `compute` method, which takes two images and returns a disparity map.

Note that it's necessary to pass rectified images as input to the `compute` method. The returned disparity map will contain per-pixel disparity values, for example, a horizontal offset in pixels between the left and right image points corresponding to the same point in the scene. That offset then can be used to restore an actual point in 3D.

When creating a disparity estimator, you can specify a number of parameters specific to the algorithm used. For a more detailed description, you can refer to OpenCV's documentation on this: `https://docs.opencv.org/master/d9/d0c/group__calib3d.html`.

There's also a module called **cudastereo** available in OpenCV that was built with CUDA support, which provides more optimized stereo algorithms. You can also check out the **stereo** module in the OpenCV contrib repository, which also contains a few additional algorithms.

The expected results are shown as follows:

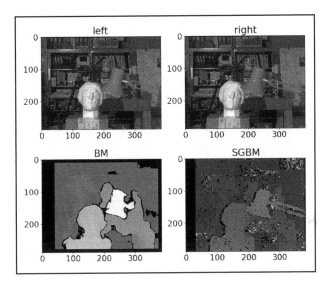

Special case 2-view geometry - estimating homography transformation

In case you need to project points from one plane to another, it's possible to do by applying a homography matrix. This matrix allows you to project a point from one plane to another if you know the corresponding transformation for the planes. OpenCV has a functionality to find the homography matrix, and this recipe shows you how to use and apply it.

Getting ready

Before you proceed with this recipe, you need to install the OpenCV version 3.3 (or greater) Python API package.

How to do it

You need to complete the following steps:

1. Import the necessary modules:

```
import cv2
import numpy as np
```

2. Load the camera matrix, the distortion coefficients, and two frames taken by the camera:

```
camera_matrix = np.load('../data/pinhole_calib/camera_mat.npy')
dist_coefs = np.load('../data/pinhole_calib/dist_coefs.npy')
img_0 = cv2.imread('../data/pinhole_calib/img_00.png')
img_1 = cv2.imread('../data/pinhole_calib/img_10.png')
```

3. Undistort the frames:

```
img_0 = cv2.undistort(img_0, camera_matrix, dist_coefs)
img_1 = cv2.undistort(img_1, camera_matrix, dist_coefs)
```

4. Find the chessboard corners on both images:

```
pattern_size = (10, 7)
res_0, corners_0 = cv2.findChessboardCorners(img_0, pattern_size)
res_1, corners_1 = cv2.findChessboardCorners(img_1, pattern_size)

criteria = (cv2.TERM_CRITERIA_EPS + cv2.TERM_CRITERIA_MAX_ITER, 30,
1e-3)
corners_0 = cv2.cornerSubPix(cv2.cvtColor(img_0,
cv2.COLOR_BGR2GRAY),
                             corners_0, (10, 10), (-1,-1), criteria)
corners_1 = cv2.cornerSubPix(cv2.cvtColor(img_1,
cv2.COLOR_BGR2GRAY),
                             corners_1, (10, 10), (-1,-1), criteria)
```

5. Find the homography between the points on both images:

```
H, mask = cv2.findHomography(corners_0, corners_1)
```

6. Apply the found homography matrix to project a point from the first image to the second one:

```
center_0 = np.mean(corners_0.squeeze(), 0)
center_0 = np.r_[center_0, 1]
center_1 = H @ center_0
center_1 = (center_1 / center_1[2]).astype(np.float32)

img_0 = cv2.circle(img_0, tuple(center_0[:2]), 10, (0, 255, 0), 3)
img_1 = cv2.circle(img_1, tuple(center_1[:2]), 10, (0, 0, 255), 3)
```

7. Transform the first image with the found homography matrix and display the result:

```
img_0_warped = cv2.warpPerspective(img_0, H, img_0.shape[:2][::-1])

cv2.imshow('homography', np.hstack((img_0, img_1, img_0_warped)))
cv2.waitKey()
cv2.destroyAllWindows()
```

How it works

To be able to project a point from one plane to another, first you need to compute the homography matrix. It can be performed with cv2.findHomography. This function accepts the following arguments:

- A set of points from the source (first) plane
- A set of points from the destination (second) plane
- A method to find homography
- A threshold to filter outliers
- An output mask for outliers
- The maximum number of iterations
- Confidence

All arguments except the first two use the default values. The method argument describes which algorithm should be used to compute the homography. By default, all points are used, but if your data tends to contain a considerable number of outliers (points with a high portion of noise or mischosen ones), it's better to use one of these methods: `cv2.RANSAC`, `cv2.LMEDS`, or `cv2.RHO`. These methods correctly filter out outliers. The threshold to filter outliers is the distance in pixels, which determines the type of the point: inlier or outlier. The mask is an object to store the values for inlier/outlier classes for each points. The maximum number of iterations and confidence determine the correctness of the solution. `cv2.findHomography` returns the found homography matrix and mask values for the points. It's also worth mentioning that you need to check that the resulting matrix is not an empty object, because a solution cannot be found for all sets of points.

After you find the homography matrix, you can apply it to the image projections by passing it to `cv2.warpPerspective`. It's also possible to project the points by multiplying them by the homography matrix (see the code).

Finally, you will see images similar to the following after executing the code:

Planar scene - decomposing homography into rotation and translation

The homography matrix can be decomposed into relative translation and rotation vectors between two plane object views. This recipe shows you how to do it in OpenCV.

Getting ready

Before you proceed with this recipe, you need to install the OpenCV version 3.3 (or greater) Python API package.

How to do it

You need to complete the following steps:

1. Import the necessary modules:

   ```
   import cv2
   import numpy as np
   ```

2. Load the camera matrix, distortion coefficients, and two photos of the same planar object (chessboard pattern). Then, undistort the photos:

   ```
   camera_matrix = np.load('../data/pinhole_calib/camera_mat.npy')
   dist_coefs = np.load('../data/pinhole_calib/dist_coefs.npy')
   img_0 = cv2.imread('../data/pinhole_calib/img_00.png')
   img_0 = cv2.undistort(img_0, camera_matrix, dist_coefs)
   img_1 = cv2.imread('../data/pinhole_calib/img_10.png')
   img_1 = cv2.undistort(img_1, camera_matrix, dist_coefs)
   ```

3. Find the corners of the pattern in both images:

   ```
   pattern_size = (10, 7)
   res_0, corners_0 = cv2.findChessboardCorners(img_0, pattern_size)
   res_1, corners_1 = cv2.findChessboardCorners(img_1, pattern_size)

   criteria = (cv2.TERM_CRITERIA_EPS + cv2.TERM_CRITERIA_MAX_ITER, 30,
   1e-3)
   corners_0 = cv2.cornerSubPix(cv2.cvtColor(img_0,
   cv2.COLOR_BGR2GRAY),
                               corners_0, (10, 10), (-1,-1), criteria)
   corners_1 = cv2.cornerSubPix(cv2.cvtColor(img_1,
   cv2.COLOR_BGR2GRAY),
                               corners_1, (10, 10), (-1,-1), criteria)
   ```

4. Find the homography matrix of transformation from the first frame to the second:

   ```
   H, mask = cv2.findHomography(corners_0, corners_1)
   ```

5. Find the possible translations and rotations for our estimated homography matrix:

   ```
   ret, rmats, tvecs, normals = cv2.decomposeHomographyMat(H,
   camera_matrix)
   ```

How it works

`cv2.decomposeHomographyMat` decomposes the homography matrix into rotations and translations. Because the solution isn't unique, the function returns up to four possible sets of translation, rotation, and normal vectors. `cv2.decomposeHomographyMat` accepts the 3x3 homography matrix and 3x3 camera matrix as arguments. The return values are: the number of found solutions, a list of 3x3 rotation matrices, a list of translation vectors, and a list of normal vectors. Each returned list contains as many elements as the number of solutions that have been found.

Rotational camera case - estimating camera rotation from homography

In this recipe, you will learn how to extract rotation from a homography transformation between two views captured by a camera undergoing only rotation motion with respect to its optical center. This is useful if, for example, you need to estimate the rotation between two views, assuming that the translation is negligible compared to distances to scene points. That's often the case in landscape photo stitching.

Getting ready

Before you proceed with this recipe, you need to install the OpenCV version 3.3 (or greater) Python API package.

How to do it

You need to complete the following steps:

1. Import the necessary modules:

   ```
   import cv2
   import numpy as np
   ```

2. Load the precomputed homography and camera parameters:

   ```
   data = np.load('../data/rotational_homography.npy').item()
   H, K = data['H'], data['K']
   ```

3. Factor out the camera parameters from the homography transformation:

```
H_ = np.linalg.inv(K) @ H @ K
```

4. Compute the approximate rotation matrix:

```
w, u, vt = cv2.SVDecomp(H_)
R = u @ vt
if cv2.determinant(R) < 0:
    R *= 1
```

5. Convert the rotation matrix to the rotation vector:

```
rvec = cv2.Rodrigues(R)[0]
```

6. Print the results:

```
print('Rotation vector:')
print(rvec)
```

How it works

In case the camera undergoes rotation only around its optical center, the homography transformation has a really simple form—it's basically a rotation matrix, but is multiplied by camera matrix parameters since homography works in image pixel space. As a first step, we factor out camera parameters from the homography matrix. After that, it must be a rotation matrix (up to scale). Since there might be noise in the homography parameters, the resulting matrix might not be a proper rotation matrix, for example, an orthogonal matrix with a determinant equal to one. That's why we construct the closest (in the Frobenius norm) rotation matrix using a singular value decomposition.

The following shows the expected results:

```
Rotation vector:
[[ 0.12439561]
 [ 0.22688715]
 [ 0.32641321]]
```

Other Books You May Enjoy

If you enjoyed this book, you may be interested in these other books by Packt:

Computer Vision with OpenCV 3 and Qt5

Amin Ahmadi Tazehkandi

ISBN: 978-1-78847-239-5

- Get an introduction to Qt IDE and SDK
- Be introduced to OpenCV and see how to communicate between OpenCV and Qt
- Understand how to create UI using Qt Widgets
- Know to develop cross-platform applications using OpenCV 3 and Qt 5
- Explore the multithreaded application development features of Qt5
- Improve OpenCV 3 application development using Qt5
- Build, test, and deploy Qt and OpenCV apps, either dynamically or statically
- See Computer Vision technologies such as filtering and transformation of images, detecting and matching objects, template matching, object tracking, video and motion analysis, and much more
- Be introduced to QML and Qt Quick for iOS and Android application development

OpenCV 3.x with Python By Example - Second Edition
Gabriel Garrido, Prateek Joshi

ISBN: 978-1-78839-690-5

- Detect shapes and edges from images and videos
- How to apply filters on images and videos
- Use different techniques to manipulate and improve images
- Extract and manipulate particular parts of images and videos
- Track objects or colors from videos
- Recognize specific object or faces from images and videos
- How to create Augmented Reality applications
- Apply artificial neural networks and machine learning to improve object recognition

Leave a review - let other readers know what you think

Please share your thoughts on this book with others by leaving a review on the site that you bought it from. If you purchased the book from Amazon, please leave us an honest review on this book's Amazon page. This is vital so that other potential readers can see and use your unbiased opinion to make purchasing decisions, we can understand what our customers think about our products, and our authors can see your feedback on the title that they have worked with Packt to create. It will only take a few minutes of your time, but is valuable to other potential customers, our authors, and Packt. Thank you!

Index

morphological operators
applying 67, 68, 69

N

natural scenes
text, detecting in 138, 139
noise
removing 53, 54
non-image data persistence
with NumPy 41, 42
non-local means algorithms
used, for denoising photo 230, 232
normalization 47
NumPy
non-image data persistence 41, 42

O

object mask
obtaining, GrabCut algorithm used 102, 103, 104, 105, 106
objects
detecting, with Single Shot Detection (SSD) model 163
finding, via template matching 111, 114
tracking, algorithms used 117, 118
OpenCV window
images, saving in 13, 14
Optical Character Recognition (OCR)
with machine learning models 129, 130, 131, 132
ORB features detector 202
orthogonal Procrustes problem 174, 175, 176, 177
Otsu algorithm
grayscale images, converting to binary images 74
output tensors' shapes
obtaining, for layers 151

P

panorama
images, stitching into 228, 230
pedestrian detector
with SVM model 127

per-element math 46
perspective transformation
image, warping 216, 219
photo
denoising, non-local means algorithms used 230, 232
pinhole camera model calibration 240, 241, 242, 243
PnP algorithm
relative camera-object pose, finding through 258, 259
points
distorting 249, 251, 252
inside of contour, verifying 90
undistorting 249, 251, 252
polynomial equations
solving 184, 185
Principal component analysis (PCA) 179, 180, 181

Q

QR code detector 140, 141, 142, 144, 145

R

rank-considerant matrix approximation
computing 177, 178
real-valued Gabor filters
images, processing with 58, 59, 60
Red, Green, Blue (RGB) 15
relative camera-object pose
finding, through PnP algorithm 258, 259
ResNet models
face detection 167
images, classifying with 159

S

Scale Invariant Feature Transform (SIFT) 199
scale invariant keypoints
detecting 199, 200
scaling values
converting 39
scene
segmenting, with Fully Convolutional Network (FCN) model 165
segment seeds